US

Everything is Done By US
We Can Make it For US

Tom Cantlon

Contents

Preface

US is a short book in plain language written that way because it is not intended to provide a full-length book experience, but to offer a thought, a way of looking at US, and nothing more.

The word "US" is generally capitalized to emphasize that we have underestimated the importance of US, and not as a reference to the U.S. With due respect to our country, where the country is referenced it is spelled out, United States, or America. The term "US" is also sometimes used in a grammatically unusual way when it is treated much like a proper name.

Punctuation is sometimes used in unusual ways. Editors made their recommendations but punctuation is sometimes used more for pacing than for accurate grammar. Pacing is used in some passages as in an impassioned speech being delivered with punch and dramatic pauses. If unusual punctuation stands out to you, try hearing it with the pauses indicated by the punctuation, but don't blame the harried editors.

Introduction

This book is about two things which tie together.

One is that we underestimate how important we are. "We" being all the regular people of the country, that is, US, as separate from powerful interests. "Powerful interests" doesn't simply mean anyone who is rich. Being rich is fine. Many people who are rich are part of US. What sets powerful interests apart is when they warp the nation in ways that are mostly for their benefit, especially in ways that leave US getting less than we should, given that we do all the work.

(If you're already wondering why "US" is always capitalized, see the note in the Preface.)

We think we need those powerful interests and are dependent on them. For instance, we think we need them to create the corporations that provide the jobs that we depend on, but the corporations would be created anyway and the jobs would exist anyway, as will be described. We do all the work that creates all the wealth that makes those corporations wealthy. In fact we do all the running of things inside those corporations that make them run. This is not a suggestion of overthrowing anyone or getting rid of anyone, it's just that we've been conned into being blind, into not seeing how

1

everything that happens, happens by US doing it. Conned into thinking we need those powerful interests when in fact they need US.

There's a lot of funding that goes into a corporation, but what does that amount to but a bunch of contracts and checks, a bunch of promises on paper, until working people, US, do the work that actually turns it into products and services, the work that actually creates the wealth.

We think we need their wealth, but in fact we, the vast numbers of everyday grocery shoppers and consumers, we are the buyers without which the corporations would have no one to sell to and no way to accumulate wealth.

We are entranced, almost hypnotized, by high tech companies that make very clever products like computers and smart phones and smart speakers in our homes that answer our questions and respond to our commands, and smart cars. We can't begin to fathom the way they work or even how they are made, how they cram so much into such tiny spaces. These companies seem almost magical, and we seem dependent on them to work that magic. But in fact every little innovative step along the way was developed by members of US. All of that innovation comes from US, as will be described.

Even people who kind of understand that we should value US more might be surprised by this one. We think we need their capital, the funding they provide to start and build and run things. We don't. In fact an enormous part of the money used for such things comes from US, as will also be described.

It's not just about money. Everything about the country is really about US. The cities and towns that have developed, the individual culture and personality of each town and area, and the civic life that holds so much of it together are all created and developed and maintained by US.

We even have the political power, though we haven't been aware of it and haven't used it. Powerful interests do have power, but we have overriding power which we just haven't used.

The country is of US, and by US. It's not even a matter of it could be by US or it should be by US. It already is, always is, of US and by US. The only thing it hasn't been is for US. It is instead too much for the benefit of powerful interests. Even that isn't because we've been overpowered, but because we've allowed it. It is a choice made by US. It's a choice we've been conned and lured into. It's a choice we can change. But first we have to know who we are. If we don't know that, there's no way we will change things. The country is of US and by US, and if we clear our heads, it can be for US.

That's the first thing.

The second thing is that there is a political approach that can make greater improvement than is normally considered. An approach that can create greater improvements for all of US, and which avoids most of the partisan differences that divide US. It avoids those divisions between US which these days have US almost equally divided. Those divisions which leave US unable to make much progress on things that would really help, and not just for some but all of US. It's a way forward that bridges that gap and therefore could harness the enormous combined power of US to make much bigger change. In fact, most of the smaller changes that could be made by either of the partisan teams would not make nearly as much difference. We can be most effective by making this change first and adding other changes that we choose later.

The goal, in one way, is hard to describe briefly because it is so broad it affects everything. In another way it is simple. It is a shift of power. A shift from the country being largely for

3

powerful interests to it being for US. It can be accomplished by a combination of top-down change and grassroots change. It requires US to actually exercise our power from the bottom up. It also needs leaders who are like-minded, either ones we choose, or by exercising the power of US to first reject current leaders and then raise up new ones from among US. Such a shift in power would not only affect national government but also state and local, and even how companies are run.

A shift in power like that wouldn't just mean that one or two big national policies are changed, but the thousands of changes that need to be made throughout the system. The thousands of laws and rules and procedures at all levels that the powerful interests have managed to bend in their favor that need to be bent back toward US. Changes that affect US not just as working people but also as consumers and as citizens.

Why would this bridge the gap between US? And what exactly are we talking about? A revolution or something? No. In fact that's part of why it doesn't raise the differences between US. It's really just going back to something we had before. Beginning just after World War II and on through the 1970s the country was run much more for US. Not perfectly, but much more than now. Unfortunately, back then all sorts of groups were excluded, which is something we don't want to go back to, but if we could recreate how that was for white men (like your author), but now have that for all of US, that would be a big step in the right direction. In fact we could make things even better than they were then, but any amount of movement in that direction is improvement, and there is nothing about moving in that direction which is revolutionary or experimental or contrary to American experience.

Things were run more for US, less for powerful interests, not just at the level of national policy, but to some extent in

4

state and local laws, and even in how companies were expected to treat their employees and their customers.

This kind of change also bridges our gap because it is a change bigger and more significant than those our partisan issues try for. A symptom of our not appreciating the importance of US is that the political solutions we hope for are puny compared to what is needed and what's possible. On the one hand, some of US might want immigration dealt with differently in hopes it would reduce jobs lost to new people, but even at best that would make a tiny difference in the overall economic health of most Americans. On the other hand, some of US might hope for some new social programs to ease problems, like some government help with child care for working people, maybe a tax break or even a straight out cash payment on child care. But there are two problems with focusing on those kinds of solutions. One is, they're not enough. If powerful interests have cut down the pay of jobs, the stability of jobs, and the consistency of hours of jobs to where it's almost impossible to work typical jobs and have kids, a little bit of help on child care isn't going to make enough difference. Stable work, on fixed hours, with all the pay that your work is really worth would get you much more than what a little help on child care can do.

The second problem is that such programs are always in reaction to some bigger problem. The overall system isn't treating people well, so we hope some social program will make it a little better. Such programs are always just a little bandage on top of a gaping wound in hopes it will slow the bleeding a little. It doesn't solve the underlying problem. F... bandages! We need real solutions. We need much bigger change than what the social programs can do for US. They're not good enough. We can do better. We need more. We can get more. But we can only get that if we focus on getting full solutions and don't make the mistake of aiming too low and just hoping for wimpy bandages.

Maybe we need different immigration policy. This book takes no position on that. Maybe some of these social programs will be needed in addition to the overall shift in power. This book takes no position on that. We can sort out those details between US. As the saying goes, it's called democracy. But something which is an option for most of US to agree on, what we could focus on, what we will have to focus on if we want more substantial change, is this shift in power, and that's something that can be participated in not just by one partisan group or another, but by all of US.

From Our Hands

After World War II people had a sense that it was US, the people, who were building a great nation, who had saved the world, and who were making these wonderful products. The sense that it was some of US, the engineers among US, who were making these great innovations. It was about US, and we were proud. Now people have more of a sense of it's all about the powerful interests, the big companies, the products that seem magical, and we are just crumbs on the table, lucky to be there. We have lost the sense of the pride we owe to ourselves for having made the amazing, rich, powerful country and economy that we have made for ourselves.

Magical Products

Part of what has caused US to lose track of our importance, in everything that is made and done, is the types of products we use these days. When a typical manufacturing job involved bolting a fender onto a car on an assembly line, we had some sense of our role in that product. These were products on a human scale. You could imagine how human hands had been involved in assembling it. You had some sense that it was people who built that. Now with products like smartphones, with circuits so tiny you need a microscope to see them, it's hard to imagine how humans had any part in creating that, other than maybe to place the circuit board in the case and close it up.

But every item that is too small to be made by hand had to first start by some person making something by hand, which was then cleverly used to scale down, smaller in each successive generation of equipment, until we had machines that could make tiny parts. But it had to start from US. Whether it's computer chips or rockets carrying astronauts—astronauts who are also part of US—we had to be involved.

It applies to the giant companies too, many of which started as tiny businesses created by someone from among US who decided to launch out into their own work.

Following are a few stories of how products built by hand led to the amazing products of today and how some of those businesses that now seem almost magical started in someone's basement. This is not meant to be a complete history or give all the details. Rather it is just to prompt our minds to remember how, in one way or another, it all has to come *from our hands*.

Steam and the early carving of metal

A good book on the whole topic of how rough, manually made, early technology was refined to the current amazing state is Simon Winchester's *The Perfectionists, How Precision Engineers Created the Modern World*. Several of the examples here he covers in great detail.

One example has to do with steam engines. Steam was vitally important in moving from handmade products to machine-made products, those that would be too hard to make by hand. Take early car engines that had to have large parts carved out of metal, something that's hard to do in any number by hand. Steam power drove the machinery in shops that could do such work. But how did the steam engines get built? They couldn't be made very well until a fellow created a way to bore out accurate cylinders, which are the heart of steam engines, in metal. And how were those cylinders carved? Using the power of water wheels. Typically, these were in a barn-sized building next to a river with a large bucket-wheel or paddle-wheel being driven by the passing river. And how were those water-wheels made? You might guess it: by hand, out of wood.

Precise measurements

The engineers in those early days of machining figured out ways to use rather crude equipment to make slightly finer equipment, which could then make yet finer equipment, so that over time they were able to make smaller and smaller parts with greater and greater accuracy. But making precise equipment requires precise measurement tools. It's kind of a chicken-and-egg problem. You need accurate tools to make accurate machines, but you need accurate machines in order to make accurate tools.

How to get started? One of the key steps was a measuring tool, a micrometer, that was amazingly accurate for its time, created in 1805. It could measure accurately and consistently down to a ten thousandth of an inch. That's roughly thirty times thinner than a human hair. The micrometer works off a long screw with very fine threads, in this case 50 threads to the inch. That's extremely fine. And this one was five feet long. How was that made? Engineer Henry Maudslay carved it out on a lathe but with only manual control, nothing to keep it precise, because there was nothing then that could create a screw so precise. As Winchester describes in his book, Maudlay tried at least forty times, each time finding the results a little off, maybe 49 threads here, 51 threads there, until finally he made one that was right along its whole length. That, in turn, allowed engineers to work much more precisely from then on. But it had to start with Maudlay and his persistent and amazing skill at manual lathe work.

Handy work in space

Let's jump forward to higher tech examples. Sometimes the tech just isn't as high as you might think. In the Air and Space Museum in Washington, DC, is the capsule that John Glenn was in when he was the first human to circle the Earth. You can look into it and see the control panel. If you look carefully you'll notice it's handmade. It's just thin sheets of aluminum that someone in a NASA (National Aeronautics and Space Administration) machine shop cut to size, drilled holes into, and attached with fat screws, probably screwed into place by hand. You might find nicer looking work in the custom dash panels of some cars that hobbyists make, but then they weren't going for looks, just for functionality. You can see pictures at the links to the Air and Space Museum. We got into space not by magic tech, but by the careful hands-on work of many of US.

The finest craft on your arm

Back to Mr. Winchester's book, he also covers how some of the most expensive watches in the world are still made by hand. The Seiko company knows how to make watches of all types and sizes, cranking them out of their factories fast and inexpensively. But their very best watches involve such fine parts and such careful assembly that they can't replicate them with machines. They still have a crew of highly skilled workers dedicated to hand assembling their best products, because it's the only way they can get it done to the level of quality they want.

Computer chips by hand

Silicon computer chips are created by placing a design of the desired circuit onto silicon and then following a process to grow that into the basic silicon that is used in the chips. But how does that design get put there in the first place? These days there are many steps done by computers, but to make the first silicon chips there were no computers to do that, certainly not ones up to doing the kind of graphic circuit design done now. It involved two steps, and they started by hand.

The way silicon chips are designed is just an extension of the way circuit boards are designed. Again, now it's done by computer, but the earliest ones were done by laying out the circuit lines with tape, as will be described. Home hobbyists can still make their own boards this way.

Black tape is laid down on clear plastic. This marks where the copper lines on the circuit board should go, connecting one component to another. This is done at a scale several times larger than what the circuit board will be. Plastic boards, which will become the circuit boards, have a solid layer of copper on top of them. There's a special light-sensitive coating over the copper. Light is shown through the clear plastic and reduced in size through lenses to project onto the circuit board. Then acid is used to eat away the copper except in the places where the wires should be, the places that didn't get exposed to light because the black tape marked these lines. The special light-sensitive coating works that way.

That's the way early electronics boards were made, especially prototypes and one-of-a-kind boards. Even later, production boards were nearly as handmade. Drafters at drafting tables would draw much neater and more precise designs which would later be projected in the same way, but the creation of the design was still a matter of hand drawing of lines where the circuits should go. Some good pictures of both the tape method and the drafting method are with the notes at the end of this book.

A little later, in 1958, when the first silicon wafers were being created, that is, whole circuits on silicon, what would be called "solid state", they used the same method. They drew out the design they wanted and then projected it by the same photographic techniques onto the silicon. Gordon Moore, the pioneer of the field, later noted that the same photo-projection technique they had used to make early circuit boards, they decided to use for making early silicon wafers. So, circuits laid out by hand. That was the start of the computer revolution.

Forging a huge metal ring

If you simply want to see an impressive example of hands creating something that seems beyond what could be handmade, there is a video link, on YouTube of course, of some men in China turning a large block of steel into a ring. It's not clear if they're making something like a train wheel, or maybe a mating ring for some huge industrial pipe fitting, but they're forming this huge, heavy ring by hand. They start with a white-hot block of steel, several feet per side. It's not entirely by hand; they do have a giant, heavy forge hammer that repeatedly drops on it to do the hammering, but it's just a dumb, straight-down drop each time. All of the shaping of it, from block to circle, to just the right thickness, to hammering the hole and cone shape required, is all guided by men using long tong tools to rapidly spin it, flip it, and manipulate it between hammer drops. It's just an impressive example of something you wouldn't have imagined could be made by hand, but they do.

Big companies from garages

It's not just technologies that sometimes seem magical; it's also the huge corporations we are impressed with. But those companies started from US, grew big by our work, and continue all they do today thanks to US. Following are just a few sample stories. The link for some of these stories was found looking for sources on Wikipedia, which is entirely appropriate since it is a volunteer, collaborative effort created by some of US.

Hewlett-Packard was started by Bill Hewlett and Dave Packard in a garage, literally. They were two electrical engineers in Palo Alto, before the area had any special claim on the electronics industry. It was 1938 and they rented a garage and started making electronic products. It's ironic that they started off with so little that between them they didn't even have a garage to use, they had to rent one. Making electronic products was fairly easy to do then since you could hand wire circuits with vacuum tubes. It was their own inventiveness that gave them a leg up to succeed. A common piece of equipment often needed for engineering work was being sold by competitors for around $200 and didn't even work that well.

Hewlett and Packard came up with a clever way to make one that was cheaper and worked better.

An early customer for the product was Walt Disney Productions. Disney was just distributing its ground-breaking *Fantasia* movie and was installing its own new sound system in theaters to make it an even more impressive event, and needed the product that Hewlett and Packard were making.

HP, as it came to be known, eventually grew into one of the largest and most innovative companies in electronics in the world.

Speaking of Disney, Roy Disney and Walt Disney started making home-made animated movies in a garage. They didn't even own the garage (much like Hewlett and Packard); it was their uncle's. Many kids still today like making their own movies with animation on paper or with stop-action toys. The Disneys were serious about it though. Within a few months they had a contract with Universal Studios to buy their animated films.

You likely know the story of Apple Computer. It was Steve Wozniak who was the initial technical driver of it, who designed its first computer. He got together with Steve Jobs, and they started the business in the garage of Jobs parents.

Amazon started a little better off. Jeff Bezos had already been a high executive in a finance company but launched off on his own in his garage, again, to start an online bookstore. Like so many tiny startups, there wasn't an actual office, so for business meetings he had to meet people at local coffee shops and, ironically, bookstores.

Google is the same thing. A couple of guys, Larry Page and Sergey Brin, had a business idea and a rented garage.

It's not all high tech though. Mattel, the toy company, started from a couple who were making picture frames at home. They decided to put some of the excess material to use to make dollhouse furniture. It progressed into all sorts of other toys from there.

Whole Foods Groceries started from a couple, John Mackey and Rene Lawson Hardy, opening a tiny store in Austin. Things were so tight that for a while they had to live in the store because they couldn't afford a place to live. Dell Computers, one of the biggest computer manufacturers in the world, was started by Michael Dell out of his college dorm room. Starbucks was started on a tiny budget by three college teachers opening one little store to sell coffee beans. EBay was created by Pierre Omidyar setting up the site on his computer in his living room. Mark Zuckerberg famously started Facebook on his computer in his college dorm room. Ben & Jerry's ice cream started in a converted gas station in Vermont. Subway Sandwiches started with two guys, Peter Buck and Fred Deluca, a tiny budget, and one store in Connecticut.

You might know the story of McDonalds. That it was started by the McDonald brothers as a little burger drive-thru. They decided to sell franchises and had a few going when Ray Kroc came along and liked the idea, bought into it, and made it really grow from there.

It is people like US who start these corporations. It is people like US who build them up. Sometimes the entrepreneur may just be smart or lucky about hiring the right people, and it is those people who come up with the ways to make a business grow. Sometimes the entrepreneur might be a real visionary who pushes things farther or is especially clever about a new business model, and those visionaries are part of the picture too, and we're glad for them. But they still started out in a

15

garage. They still needed an army of US to support and carry out their cleverness. Apparently, we do it very well, judging by how these companies have grown.

Valuable innovations

Even when companies get big or start off big because some powerful interests formed a company, the magic that comes out of them still comes from US. Here are just a couple of examples, well-known stories of people discovering product ideas.

A Swiss mechanical engineer named George de Mestral was working for an engineering company back in the 1940s when he came upon the idea for Velcro. It occurred to him separately from his work, because of the burs that stuck to his clothes when he hiked. He examined the tiny hooks in the burs and got the idea. It took him many years, but he eventually managed to develop a practical way to manufacture it, patented it, and then form his own company to sell it.

A more typical story is the Raytheon Corporation and its invention of the microwave oven. This was during the period of World War II and the years after. Raytheon was a big government contractor for defense projects. The corporation had been developing and producing microwave radar for tracking enemy planes. As a side development it invented the microwave oven. This was a seemingly magical thing. You can imagine, as this was the time before anything like it had been seen. TV was still new, and many people still used wood in stoves to cook, and here was this magical box that in couple of minutes could make cold food hot. The early ones impractical, large and expensive, but still Raytheon could claim to be bringing this magic to any home that could afford it.

But did Raytheon create this magic? Yes and no. It was a combination of the existence of Raytheon and its research for defense and one of US, an engineer named Percy Spencer. Percy was very knowledgeable and innovative about microwaves. That's why Raytheon hired him. It was a collaboration. Percy made Raytheon look good and make money by making Raytheon look like the inventor of various advances in microwaves, and Raytheon was a place with the facilities and funds where Percy could pursue his innovations.

While working with microwaves he noticed things would get hot, like a candy bar in his pocket would melt. He was observant enough and curious enough to pursue this, and knowledgeable enough to know how. With some experiments he figured out how to confine the microwaves in a metal box and heat up things in it.

Here's the typical scenario of how an inventor like Percy in a big company like Raytheon works. Percy was paid a salary to do research. He probably had a contract, which is common for this kind of work, so that any invention or valuable discovery he came up with, while employed by Raytheon, immediately became the property of Raytheon. Typically, this even covers inventions dreamed up outside of work, on the theory that they may have been inspired by work. This is also so that the inventors can't just claim they did it outside of work. Raytheon got the patent and the profit. Percy got his salary.

Actually, Percy eventually did well. He became a high executive in Raytheon and did much more in the field. Any company that's smart will find some way to reward its inventors or when their contract is up they'll just go somewhere else. Still, this is how these seemingly magical companies create their magic. The companies play an important part too, by providing the facilities and tools and by hiring skilled people and letting them do their work. But ultimately it comes down to people, US, creating the magic.

Sometimes it can be big steps, like Percy and his microwave oven, and sometimes it can be a lot of little steps, like the assembly line supervisor who sees a change that could make assembly quicker and easier, and then that company has an advantage over their competitors.

For a small company to grow very big, or for a big company to stay big, and if that happens because they really do things better, it takes an accumulation of a lot of innovations and advances and things done right. And all of those things are not some magic that just appears out of the company. They are all done by US.

Apple, the Macintosh, and the iPhone

Apple, Inc. might seem like the most magical company with the most magical products, but dig a little deeper and it's really the best example of the work of US.

Two examples. The first is about the Macintosh. It was famously the first popular, successful computer with a graphic user interface and a mouse. Before that, personal computer screens just had text, no graphics, and you typed in what you wanted them to do. People can't be blamed for thinking that Apple, famously led by Steve Jobs at the time, invented the graphic system and the mouse, but the development of each involves a lot more of US.

The invention of the mouse was preceded by the trackball, a sort of upside-down mouse with a large ball on which the user placed on open hand in order to roll it in a given direction. That in turn moved the cursor on a screen. It was first invented by a British engineer, just after World War II, about 1946, for use in radar systems.

In 1963, in America, an engineer at Stanford Research Institute thought of something similar but flipped the design, so the ball would be on the table and move as the hand moved the mouse. A few years later a German company offered a mouse-like device with one of their computers.

In the early 1970s Xerox started selling the first computer intended to be a one-person, one-workstation computer, sort of the first personal computer. It included a mouse.

In 1982 Microsoft made their program Word able to use a mouse. It was still text based, but you could move the mouse to move the cursor.

Then, after all of that, it was in 1984 that Apple started to sell the Macintosh.

The Macintosh had more than just a mouse; it had the graphic user interface, the graphic icons on the desktop which you could use the mouse to interact with. It was the first popular computer that could do things like let you grab a document icon with the mouse and drag it to the trashcan icon.

But that didn't start with the Macintosh. Before that, Apple had briefly sold the Lisa computer, which was similar but expensive and never sold many.

The Lisa was inspired by work done at Xerox by the same engineers who had developed the mouse for their computer. They had for several years been working on a graphic user interface or GUI. Steve Jobs and some Apple engineers saw this work in 1979 and made an agreement with Xerox. From that, a team of engineers at Apple developed the ideas of the GUI and mouse into the finished Lisa product.

From Our Hands

When the Lisa and then the Macintosh came out, Microsoft engineers had already been working on Microsoft Windows. Their first version came out shortly after the Macintosh but was very limited, sort of a bit of graphics added on top of the text-based DOS systems. It took until about 1990 for them to create a version that started to become popular.

So the mouse evolved by various engineers over decades, and the GUI was largely invented by the engineers at Xerox. The Apple team then advanced it and turned it into a product.

Apple's other most famous product is the iPhone, or, to use the generic term, the smartphone. Like the GUI and mouse, you can't blame people for thinking Apple invented it, but the smartphone was created in steps by engineers at numerous companies over years.

The first product that could be called a smartphone was demonstrated in 1992 and started sales in 1994. It was developed by an engineer at IBM. It was a large, bulky phone with a touch pad which you could use to send email, take notes, and get some news. Lots of companies made products in the following years that improved on it. Some of these companies had for years been making products that were similar to the early smart phone, only without the phone. They were digital data devices that could take notes, keep calendars, and communicate that information, in and out, to other similar devices or to computers. Some could communicate via email and text. The market for those quickly adapted to combine those devices together with the cell phones of the time.

Over the next decade these devices evolved, and design teams at many companies made versions: Palm, Hewlett-Packard, Nokia, Qualcomm, Ericson, Kyocera, and Blackberry, as well as companies that produced and sold products mostly in Japan. It wasn't until 2007 that Apple released its iPhone.

Apple, which is perhaps the company that seems most nearly magical, and its two flagship product categories, the Macintosh and the iPhone, two products that most exemplify almost magical products, gained such success by leaning on the work of US. The various leaders of Apple deserve credit for foreseeing the most popular directions that tech was going to go, and gathering up those of US whose skill and innovation were developing those technologies, and combining those people together to develop products quicker than the competition did. They deserve credit. But what they can accurately be credited with is being good at making the most out of the work of US.

We Don't Need Them, They Need US

Really? We don't need them? Really? They need US? Yep, really. They need US in six keys ways that are covered here.

We tend to think our economy is dependent on our having the big players. We've been conned into thinking that, but that is exactly backwards.

Most of the talk about the economy looks at it from the top down. It's all about "job creators", and when taxes are cut, they're cut for the top on the theory that will lead to investment and more jobs and be good for people. Back in the 1980s this was referred to as "trickle down". Eventually, use of that term faded both because it was constantly shown that it didn't work and because it was too obviously just a ploy, an excuse for the top to treat themselves ever better and try to get you to believe that it's for your benefit. That term might not be used much anymore, yet still when we hear the daily news and hear some segment about corporations and hear them referred to as "job creators" we tend to think, yes, thank goodness they're creating jobs. Our heads are still locked into thinking about the economy in those top-down, "thank goodness we have the top

23

to create our jobs for us", ways. It's the same trickle-down theory but without using that term, and it's locked inside our very own heads. Let's look at six key aspects of the economy and see if it's true that the economy works from the top down.

Six Ways That the Economy is All About US

Wealth

Wealth is the first way. How is wealth created? One is by someone pulling together a business. It takes mountains of cash to start up a big operation, it takes shiploads of raw material if you are going to make much of anything, and it takes some kind of assembly operation. But all of that would be nothing, the mountains of cash would be worth no more than mountains of paper, the raw materials nothing more than that, just raw, the assembly operation idle, until you get the labor of the employees into the picture. Wealth is created as a partnership between someone who pulls those things together and the employees, the laborers, the strength of the people who actually take those raw materials and turn them into something worthwhile. Without those people doing that, the idea of the business is just an idea. It's that partnership with US that makes wealth.

In fact, stating that "someone pulls these things together" overstates it. If it's anything larger than just a few people, if some new corporation, or some new venture of some company, is going to start something like a manufacturing plant and make a lot of money off of it, it's going to be a big operation to "pull these things together", just to get the factory ready, much less running. In fact, it's going to be a big operation just to plan whether it can be done profitably, to investigate financing options, to consider plant designs, to scout locations. It's going to take secretaries and administrators and assembly line designers and engineers and purchasing agents and all sorts of people who actually carry out the vision of the one with the idea. It's all of them who have to know how to do their part and do it well, or the idea never comes together. So that person with an idea and that large team of people to carry it out, "pull these things together", and even then they just have a factory ready, but not running until it's filled with employees.

Sometimes you visit someone's home and you say, "This is a nice home" and they say, "Thank you. We built it". Generally, they don't really mean they built it. They mean they contracted it. They mean they had an idea. They either had the money or the credit-worthiness to get a loan, and they bought the land and hired a contractor, maybe found an architect, and a home was built, but not by them. It was built by laborers, by skilled people, by a contractor, by carpenters who've who spent many years doing carpentry and know what kind of wood is good for various places. They know what kind of insulation and weathering is going to be needed in this environment. They've seen over the years other carpenters and contractors cut corners and they've seen what happens with those houses over time. They know what's good and they are skilled. They have the necessary knowledge and they work hard. They go out there early in the morning when it's cold and disregard the cold and just dig in and start turning a pile of boards into a house. It is the laborers who create that. The resulting house is now valuable. That's how wealth is created. It's either created by one of US who brings a bunch more of US together to make the whole thing happen, or it can be a collaboration with some big corporation or rich entrepreneur, but which then needs a lot of

US to make it happen, and the whole process is heavily dependent on US.

Entrepreneurs

That brings us into the second item, entrepreneurs, the people who start their own businesses. They can be tiny one-person businesses or big ventures that are simply new. This is a mixed point where the big players sometime have an important role, but it's also true that they're not required.

Sometimes experienced big-business people start new companies or new product lines within their company, or someone who has a lot of their own wealth does it. That's good. It's one of the ways that the things that people need and want get made. Other times the big companies miss what people want and it's a small start-up that meets the need, such as tiny little Apple Computer, when it was first starting, being the classic example. That's also one of the ways big companies become big. Many of the biggest companies today that seem to offer such wonderful products actually bought those products from small start-up companies. It's a common pattern among big tech companies that they offer products in some particular field, say, operating systems like Microsoft Windows or social media platforms or business software, but they miss at providing all of the features their users want. So some little startup company creates an add-on product or a similar or parallel product, and it starts to grow, enough to prove that it's a valuable product line. Then the big company, wanting to keep as much control of the field as possible and keep as much of the profit in its field as possible, buys up the start-up and incorporates the new product into their big company. Or the other way they do it is to create their own version of the product or service and drive the little innovator out of business.

In each of those situations it's a small entrepreneur who should get the credit. Where the product ends up owned by a big company, it's another case of how these big companies that offer seemingly magical products once again owe what they do to small developers. They owe it to some of US.

Even when some brilliant new business venture or product line comes entirely from some big player or big existing company, is it just some brilliant CEO or executive who does that? The leaders might have some wonderful creative input in some cases, and that's great. In other cases, they might only know that they need something. For instance that the company is already selling all it can of some product and it needs to come up with new related products, or that the company needs a new marketing approach, or that the company or the entrepreneur has a lot of money to invest and they would like to find some good business venture to put it into. Do the leaders figure out the details for themselves? Or do they have their people dig into it for them? They call in the marketing staff to brainstorm some new marketing approaches. They canvas the engineers to see what related innovations they might have as possibilities. Or they look outside the company to see what related innovations independent inventors have already patented and are offering for sale. Or if they're looking for some entirely new business to start, they can again turn to advisers to scour the market trends and help them find what business looks like the best to go into.

You know in the movie *The Wizard of Oz*, when the characters finally get to see the wizard, and they see an image of his floating head surrounded by smoke and lights and scary noise? The wizard had a role to play, but it wasn't magic. It was smoke machines and light displays and booming sound systems that made him seem magical. Did he invent the smoke machine? Or build it himself? Not likely. It's all the hard work and cleverness of many munchkins behind the scenes.

In articles in business newspapers and news sites, it's not unusual to find corporate leaders complaining that any new taxes or new regulations will cut into their profit margin, and that in turn will make it just not worth expanding business or starting new ventures. Of course, partly they're just trying to push scare stories to discourage legislators from adding any taxes or regulations, but they also truly mean it could cut into profits and make them wonder whether they want to bother doing more, and that in turn might mean fewer jobs created. But what is considered worth doing by any given investor is a relative notion. Many of the biggest industries and the most successful companies have become accustomed to high rates of profit. If they think that high rate might get a little lower, down to a more middling rate of profit, they might just find it not worth doing, take their huge personal wealth, and go home and just sit on their money and place it in some safe stock market investments. But what might not seem worthwhile to them might seem great to some of the hungrier, smaller-scale entrepreneurs in the field who are eager for a chance to grow into the field in any gap where the big players leave an opening. Whatever the field, if the big players don't want to play, there's almost certainly someone smaller eager to fill that need.

Sometimes the big corporation develops a new line, or the rich, experienced entrepreneur does. That's one way business supplies what people need, but clearly it's not the only way. It's not the required way. As far as starting or expanding business, the big players are a welcome part of the picture but not required. Sometimes they have important roles to play, then sometimes it's really more the people working for them who have the innovations. And sometimes when the big players miss what's needed or just don't play, it's the smaller innovators who fill the need. We are not dependent on them, and when the big ways of doing things don't do it, the required ingredient comes back to what it always comes back to, US.

Supply

The third item is supply. When there is a need to ramp up the supply of some kind of product, when we suddenly need to make more of something, then existing companies, especially large ones, can sometimes be very good at ramping up production quickly. But sometimes they don't. Sometimes they just misunderstand the market for a product, or sometimes they just don't know that there's a market for a product at all. Maybe the public is ready for a new innovation that the big companies miss, and sometimes it takes the small entrepreneurs to fill the need.

Way back when, there were a couple of brothers in San Bernardino who started a little burger joint and figured it could be spread like crazy, and they developed it into McDonald's. It can be a couple of guys in a garage who think that the existing computer companies are missing the mark on what the market really wants, and they grow to be Apple Computer.

And it doesn't even have to be the case of entrepreneurs starting a little thing that grows into something huge. Often times it is the huge number of small players who fill a need. Most of the homes that are built in the country are built by small contractors. It's a lot a small independent businesses that build most of these homes. In a sense they build the nation. It is not built by some big corporation or a handful of big corporations. It's built by a million small contractors. Same thing with the million independent dentists or landscapers or accountants or a thousand other categories. That's where supply comes from. It comes either from the big players bringing in a bunch more of US to ramp up production, or sometimes from some of US taking the bull by the horns and just making it happen.

Capital

The fourth thing is capital, the money needed to do any of these things. Now that's a part of the economy where clearly we need the rich, the big players, the big banks and financiers. Right? No. We don't. No, we don't. The money to start or expand some operation can come from a few big investors or it can come from many small ones, and often does. Very often. Even companies that have tons of money, for various reasons, when they go to do some big expansion, generally don't spend their own money. Generally they borrow money.

Companies choose where to borrow depending on their size. In small operations they go to the local bank. Bigger operations have to go to bigger banks or sell stock or take in more investors. Do you think all of those investors are big players? No. Where does the bank get a lot of the money that it has for lending out? From the million-and-one small savers. From everyone from the Warren Buffetts down to the people who are just barely getting by and it's a miracle they can save anything, but by goodness they're determined to save some money. So they save a little out of each paycheck, and that goes into a savings account, and that gets loaned out by the bank.

And it's not just bank loans. Who are the big investors that do a lot of big stock buying, the big investors who end up owning significant portions of companies? Some of the biggest players in investing are pension funds and mutual funds, and they are big players. But where do they get such big money to invest? From the million and one little people they represent. Mutual funds take in money from some big players and many small players. Much of the money in pension funds comes from the small amounts out of every paycheck that people direct into their pension savings. Many of the other big pools of money come from outfits that represent many small players. Insurance companies have to keep tons of money available so they can pay out against big claims when there's a hurricane or other disaster. They have to have enough money available, but they also invest it to make it grow, and so they end up being huge players in the finance world. But where does all that money come from? From US. From the premiums we all pay on home insurance and every other kind of insurance. It then belongs to the insurance companies and they take their profit, but they have to hold an enormous amount of it for US and invest it for US so that it's available to pay back to US when we are hit with disasters.

All of the money held by everyone, rich and poor, goes into one big pool of money that all mixes together and becomes the total pool of money that is available to be invested. Invested into new business and employment and growth. Consider this. If you could magically flip a switch and instantly have every employee in the country suddenly get 10 percent more pay, and in turn every profitable company got 10 percent less profit, and every wealthy owner or investor got 10 percent less income, so that more of it went to employees, it wouldn't change the total amount of money in the country at all. It's just that rather than so much of it being in the huge bank accounts of the top, a little more of it would be in each little bank account of workers. It would all still be the same pool of money, and just as big of a pool either way, just a little less in the big accounts and a little more in the little accounts. Businesses and entrepreneurs, both big and small entrepreneurs, looking to find funding from the banks and other finance sources would still find just as much money available, because it's all still part of the same big pool.

You may have heard the supposedly clever phrase, "You've never gotten a job from a poor person". Yes, you have. If that poor person has even one dollar saved in the bank and that bank loaned money to the company you work for to start or grow, then, yes, you have gotten a job in part from that poor person, and from a whole bunch more of US, the typical, small-account, working people.

We don't need the rich to have the money to start or grow business. The money can come from a few rich people or from the pooled money of the many of US, and more often it is from that big pool of all of US. The money to do things comes from all of US.

Labor

The fifth part is the labor itself. Despite technological advances and outsourcing and such, when an economy is doing well, it takes darn near everyone who's capable of working to be working. To create a nation's worth of sufficient wealth takes many, many hands. We certainly can't rely on a few big players to provide that. It takes the many.

Demand

Finally, the sixth part of the economy is demand. Demand is the people out there wanting to buy things, with money in hand ready to make purchases.

Rich people buy more than the average person, and they buy more expensive stuff, but there are lots of things where there's just kind of a human limitation on how much they buy. Even if someone had a million times the wealth of the ordinary person (yes, there really are a few of them), who maybe owns ten homes and every home has ten bedrooms, they still only need 200 pillows on those beds. They are not going to buy a million pillows because they have a million times the wealth. To have a healthy economy, almost by definition, the key thing is to have a lot of demand. In order to have a lot of demand it takes pretty much everyone in the economy having money. Money they can use to go out and buy the things that they need and want in order to have a reasonable standard of living. It won't do any good to have a handful of people who buy a few hundred pillows and then have millions of other people who don't have the money to buy one. We need everybody who needs pillows to have the money to go out and buy them.

The way they get money is to have jobs, good-paying jobs. But even more so, they need jobs that make for a stable middle-income living. Jobs that are steady and long term, that they can grow with, and that have retirement plans. Those kinds of jobs.

It is the demand of the many that creates enough total demand, enough to make a thriving economy. And it is demand that is often the piece that's missing. That is the key thing. That's what creates jobs. Companies can't start or grow unless there are people who will buy their product. On the other hand, if there's some product or service that people want more of, you can bet someone will start or grow a company to fill that demand and therefore get the profit from doing that. Starting or growing a company to fill some need requires, what? Employees. So it is demand that really is the driving creator of jobs. And demand comes from all of US having the income to purchase a decent way of life. It's a wonderful self-fulfilling cycle. Pay people well and they'll have the money to buy stuff. Their buying of stuff leads to the creation of more jobs.

Major companies and major investors are sitting on record amounts of cash. They're investing it in very low-yield investments because there just isn't more demand. They could invest it in making bigger factories, but only if there are more people with money out there ready to buy what they would make. If there aren't enough people out there with enough money then they can't build bigger factories, so they have to find other ways to invest their money. Other ways that generally don't pay as much as selling their product, if only there were more people with more money able to buy.

For those companies to have all this money on hand available to them, and not be able to invest it in increased production which would give a really good rate of return? It's excruciating. They want to make their money work, to make it grow. It's like a drag racer revved up and ready to explode off the starting line, but the starting light just won't light. The race car is the abundance of supply that's ready to spring into action, but demand is the light that just won't light.

You can be 100 percent certain that the moment these companies that are sitting on record amounts of cash, the moment they think there is more demand for whatever their product is, they will ramp up production and the jobs that go with that, so they can make more money. Regulations be darned. Taxes be darned. If there's better profit to made from production rather than having their money sit in safe but not-very-profitable investments, they'll climb over each other trying to be the first to get more production out there. What's standing in the way is there aren't enough people out there with enough money wanting to buy the product. Demand is missing. Enough money in the hands of the millions of people who would otherwise go out and buy stuff is missing. Without demand, nobody's going to ramp up production, nobody's going to hire people. It's a self-fulfilling downward cycle when demand is less than what it would be if we were all receiving our full value.

In each of those six aspects, the roles that we each play take on all forms, from the carpenter to the office administrator to the high-level manager and even the CEO, and we need all of them to be doing what they're good at. We're all in this economy together. The labor of all can be honored. There's nothing biased against the CEO or the big investor in this view from the bottom up. What there is, is reality. And the reality is that we are not dependent on the big players; the big players are dependent on the millions of little people. They need our labor, they need our purchasing, they need our capital.

We need to break this notion, this almost hypnotic notion, that we are dependent on what's big. The opposite is true.

There's nothing in the free-market system that requires big, wealthy, powerful players to make it work. This nation started off largely as a farming economy, with the people who came over here on ships mostly just having what little they could bring with them. Yet somehow we built up from there into an industrial nation. It's because the little people, those farmers, the individual businesses, the entrepreneurs, built up from there. It is because it is possible to build from small up to big.

It is the small that's needed and can build up to the big. It is the small end of the spectrum that is important. It is the massive wealth creation of millions and millions of people going to work every day and doing productive stuff that makes us a wealthy nation.

Not just economic wealth, but social fiber, strength as a nation. It includes people who are working but not at a paid job. If a couple decides that one spouse is going to stay home and make sure the kids get a good start, they're both contributing to the strength of that family, that household. That, in turn, contributes to the strength not only of the economy, but of their community, the society. It is the strength of the many doing their jobs that makes a strong country. It is all of those people, it is the small end of the spectrum, it is the small contributions of the millions that create the real strength of this economy.

If you look at each of those points above, one thing is clear about every key aspect of the economy. It's...all...about...US. A healthy economy needs US, is about US, is dependent on US, and all the work that makes it happen comes from our hands.

The shift to thinking it's about US and by US is almost like trying to help someone who has gotten lured into a cult to break free from the mind control of it. Someone in a cult might think that what the cult does is good work and essential and it would be horrible if the members left the cult. That's uncomfortably close to how we often think of the wealthy and powerful as people that we need or we wouldn't have jobs.

Someone in a cult might think the cult leaders, who've gotten wealthy and live comfortably while the members sacrifice and give, that those leaders are doing good things and if the members leave, how would those leaders continue to have the money to do their good work? That's uncomfortably close to how we think that if anything diminishes the wealth of the wealthy it will hurt the economy when in fact some changes, like higher wages, would make it a better and fairer economy. Someone in a cult might think that if they had to leave they wouldn't know how they'd live, where they'd sleep, who would feed them, who would provide for them, when in fact they're capable of building their own life and would be better for it. That's uncomfortably close to how we think that the wealthy and big corporations not only are the source of jobs, but we think they are the source of the capital to run the economy. We think they are the source of the products we need, when, in fact, we are the ones who do all of that, and we would be better off for being more aware of that. We would all be better off for running the economy and the country in general with that in mind.

Several themes in this book come up multiple times in part because we are locked into those thinking patterns that we need to see clearly and change. It's also because the themes all tie together and when one aspect is looked at it leads to seeing how the other parts tie to it. But it's partly because of that almost cult-like thinking that is hard to become fully aware of. It takes some practice, some repetition, to get used to looking at things in a truer way.

That our minds are locked into some thinking ruts is not surprising. It's normal human behavior. If you're raised and live all your life in a culture that constantly tells you and gives you the understanding that certain things are truths, then your mind gets locked into thinking that way. It's not surprising that powerful interests push these ideas. Even when powerful interests aren't intending to be deceptive, they're going to promote their own interests, like anyone does. Only their wealth makes them much better able to push things in their direction. It's not a surprising situation, but it's not one we need to buy or accept or fail to push back on. We can correct our own thinking, see the reality more clearly, and encourage our fellows to do the same.

So why aren't we in charge? Why aren't we receiving our full value? Why aren't things run the way we want so that they work out well for US and for the priorities that we want to focus on? That's what this book is about. It's about how it's in our hands to change that.

Who Are Part of US, and Who Aren't

So who exactly is included in US? Very roughly speaking, US are darn near all of US, almost all of the people, the regular work-a-day people. The only ones who are not part of US are people who have enough powerful influence to be harmful to US, and who actually do things harmful to US. So does that mean everyone who is rich or who is influential is not part of US? Is it that kind of "US against them"? Not at all.

The rich and the powerful can be part of US, if they will be. The skilled CEOs who can run a big corporation are part of the team. We need all of the positions, from top to bottom, all of the people doing their jobs for things to run well. Someone who rises to great wealth by legitimate means and who is not busy trying to use that wealth and influence to squeeze those of lesser income just so the person at the top can have even more, someone of wealth who is fully on-board with the average worker getting the full value of their work, by all means, they're part of US. Wealth and influence are not the dividing lines.

Who Are Part of US

The dividing line has more to do with those who would endlessly squeeze lower earners to get more for themselves. Those with no regard for others getting the full rewards that they should.

There are two ways that kind of disregard for others can show up. One is simple greed and indifference. The other is people who have a particularly low opinion of US. That is, people who think that there is some huge percentage of US who are lazy and living fat and happy off of food stamps or short-term unemployment checks (as if). Their attitude leads to business groups and legislators wanting to change the rules so that unemployment checks end even sooner. They think that, no doubt, people are refusing to take jobs because they're having too much fun on their tiny unemployment checks, so let's cut them off because surely they are such lowly people that that's the only way to get them to work. Both kinds of disrespect for US result in actions that harm US.

That attitude of disrespect is one aspect of it. The other aspect is being in a position to actually do something about it, being someone who either makes laws and rules or can strongly influence them, and being someone who uses that influence to harm those who have less income or influence.

That aspect of having exceptional power to harm others is important because, someone who is just an ignorant S.O.B. who wishes open racism was legal again, but who is just an ignorant individual working to get by, and isn't part of any active supremacist group by night, is still one of US. An ignorant, loathsome member, but still having the right to their ignorant opinion, and still one of US. If they become head of even a modest size company and refuse to hire anyone but their own race, or purposely hire people who are easily intimidated so they can underpay them, then they would become someone who is not one of US.

It's possible for people to not be aware they are working against US. If, say, they have a large company and they lobby their representative to pass some proposed tax break and don't realize it gives the big companies an unfair advantage and hurts the mom and pop shops. Or someone has actually convinced them it would be a favor to unemployed people to kick them off of unemployment benefits, and they lobby for that. For some, just being a little more aware might make the difference, but in the meantime they are using their influence in ways that harm US.

Defining "working people"

In this book, references to US are often mixed interchangeably with references to working people, but "working people" is a much broader group than it might at first seem. It includes people currently working a job, people looking for work, those training for some future work, those on an extended break from work because they've earned the ability to do that, people who work just enough at jobs to get by because they have other non-paid work they feel is important, like pursuing their artistic passion or volunteering in all sorts of ways, people rich enough to not have to work but who choose to make themselves constructive parts of the community, people pursuing a life of spirituality because that's how they think they can do the most good, the retired who've completed their work-life, and the stay-at-home spouses who chose to focus on raising the kids well and other family goals. It also includes those who are our people: our children, our disabled family and relations, our elderly. Working people, in this broader sense, means darn near everyone.

The actively prejudiced

People who are not just prejudiced but are serious supremacists or some other "my tribe only" group are also not part of US. It makes for another fuzzy dividing line, but it's important, and here's why.

Someone who is fearful of the unknown and just doesn't know what to make of people of other colors or other cultures, or someone who used to find their town full of people just like them and now it has a lot of "others" and it's just less comfortable to them, or someone who was raised prejudiced, is just that, simply prejudiced. Subtle prejudice is something many of US have been raised with. We may find some of it within ourselves no matter who we are or what our background is. It's something most of US would like to grow out of when our eyes are open to seeing it in ourselves.

On the other hand there are those who actively want a nation that is flatly not about democracy or rights. They want a nation that is simply tribal, and run of, by, and for themselves and people of their group. Once someone joins a group or actively tries to turn the nation into one that is just for some people, they're into very un-American ideas, ideas that are against US and against American principles.

So, those who are not part of US are those of simple greed or those with an ignorant superior attitude and who are in positions to harm us, and those who are pursuing a clearly un-American system.

The rest are US: the noble and not so noble, saints and sinners, wealthy and poor, those of a strong mind and stable emotions and upbringing that gave them discipline and drive, and those of unclear mind, roller-coaster emotions, and bad influences, but who can, and do, earn their keep. Plus those who have worse problems and are flat out incapable of earning their keep, and we carry them, because they are ours. They're part of US. US includes those who are very industrious, and the surf-bum who does just enough odd jobs to support their hobby, but who legitimately does earn their keep.

US are everyone who isn't trying to prevent regular people getting what they're due.

Those who are working against US by power and influence or by hatred are not US.

Prejudice, the Ins and Outs, and Identity Politics

Prejudice against any ethnicity, skin color, gender of all variations, sexual preference, or any other group just for who they are is immoral, deserving of our anger, enormously damaging, and ignorant.

At the same time we are not going to get rid of all those who are prejudiced or cure them all tomorrow, and it's going to take all of US to achieve making the country for US. Like it or not, US includes prejudiced people.

Identity politics

Identity politics is a term used to describe when any group who are being harmed try to end the damage being done to them. They might be a group by skin color or gender or sexual preference, or just a group who have been taken advantage of, like low-wage workers, or a more specific group like home care workers or hotel room cleaners. Some people are critical of focusing on identity politics issues because they think it splinters US from working together. Others feel it's necessary

45

as the only way to end problems encountered by this or that group. We need both. We need to work together to have the leverage for broad change, and we need to make sure each group that's being harmed has that stop. There's no need to choose one way or the other.

The whole point of making the country be for US is just that, for it to be for all of US. The work that we do to make the country be for US cannot be separated from the work that we do to end inequality. They have to go together. We need the country to be for US, and at the same time to gain equality for every slighted group, to have the damage against them ended, and to restore absolutely equal status. Equal not just in concrete tangible things like equal pay, but also in respect. Not just status as a group tolerated to be here, or even as a nicely treated subgroup, but full status to be just as able to be in positions of leadership. A country that is for almost all of US but is not for this or that group, has not achieved becoming a nation for US.

Actually, there can be no separating of these two goals. Consider a black woman as an example. She would identify as black and participate in efforts to end unequal treatment of black people, but at the same time she's a member of a subgroup within that. She's a woman. She would participate in efforts to end unequal treatment of women. She wouldn't give up pursuing one goal while she works on the other. In fact, it would do her little good to succeed in ending one kind of damage while she continues to suffer the other kind. In the same way we cannot just focus on raising the status of most of US but ignore the prejudice against any subgroup. We need to be clear, and keep it prominently clear, that making things right for US means making things right for all of US. If we improve things for many of US but not for those of US of color or those of US who are women or those of US who are gay or whatever group, then we haven't really made the nation for US.

White people have often participated in efforts to end prejudice against skin color. If you look back on photos of marches and rallies led by Martin Luther King Jr. and other notable leaders of that civil rights era, you'll see plenty of white people in the mix. And you can look up the numbers on the overwhelming majority of men who support the equal rights amendment for women. That's who we need to be, those people who pull for one another. It's the only way we can achieve success for US.

The prejudiced as part of US

Prejudice can be separated into intentional and unintentional. Almost all of us have at least some small amount of prejudice. For many of us, though, it's something we don't like about ourselves and we try to change it when we see it arise in ourselves. If that's all the prejudice there was, it would be a much smaller problem and one we would improve on over time.

Then there are those who are intentionally prejudiced, strongly prejudiced, actively prejudiced. Even short of those who openly spout white nationalist or similar hatred are those who are actively prejudiced in how they live and have no desire to change that. People who won't hire or rent to or deal with any but what they think is their own kind. F… them. They deserve our anger. The damage they do is so monumental we can't begin to wrap our heads around it.

Unfortunately, there are a lot of them and, as noted, we can't get rid of them or change them in a hurry. They are part of US. We are a flawed bunch. There are plenty of US who are

The Prejudiced

members of the groups who are slighted, who are the targets of prejudice, yet who are prejudiced themselves. It's understandable when a member of a group who is held down is prejudiced against the group doing the holding down, but it still does tremendous damage. But plenty of times it doesn't even make sense, like when a member of one slighted group, for unexplainable reasons, is prejudiced against members of another slighted group. Prejudice shows up in all of our subgroups and comes in all flavors.

But even looking beyond just prejudice, many of US who don't have that particular sin have other sins against other people. Many of US have flaws in how we treat our families, our relationships, in our shortcomings in honesty. It's human. Some of US do much better than others, but we can't make a nation that is only of, by, and for the nearly flawless. It is precisely we humans, flaws and all, who have the right to make our own nation to be of, by, and for US. All of US.

Keep in mind that prejudice may get worse under worse conditions. People who work against US getting our full due create conditions that, in turn, lead some of US, those of shaky principles, to turn to prejudice as a way to make sense of the world. It gives people who are frustrated a target to direct their frustration at. Working to regain our proper power and full respect may lessen the pressure to resort to prejudice.

What does it mean to accept that some of US are prejudiced as we work to regain our proper power? It does not mean that we should tolerate their prejudice. We should still counter-rally against rallies for racial supremacy or whatever kind of hatred is being pushed. We should still counter it in private conversations when someone says something that's prejudiced. Hate their hatred or pray for them or whatever you're inclined to do. But even from among those who voted in the past for candidates spouting prejudice, those people can still, now, be part of US, if they will. They can be part of our refocusing the nation for US.

It doesn't mean they can have their ideas in some platform of demands by US. It doesn't mean racial supremacists or any other prejudice group can march as a group with their banners and literature in our parade. We don't need to tolerate their hatred, and yet those who are prejudiced can work with US on those areas where we have common goals, like economic issues that affect US all.

It's a gray, muddy problem, trying to completely reject prejudice, yet we need US to be all of US to succeed. There is no clean answer. It's just one more way the damn people who are openly prejudiced make a mess of things. What we can do is err toward rejection. We need their votes and their support to move our common goals forward, like better pay for all, but any time it gets tangled up with their prejudice, forget it. Better to move slower, but without that sin.

It's just one of the more embarrassing and darker aspects of human nature that, like it or not, the prejudiced are part of US.

Working Peoples' Share Is Declining

Here's a perfect example of the problem, and a piece of the solution. It gets into a few numbers but you don't need to follow the details, just the general idea that this problem is costing you a lot of money. And know that the underlying reason that our share has been declining is all about a loss of power on our part. Likewise, the fix has nothing to do with taxing or social programs or limiting the rich or any of the usual controversial ideas. That's because what went wrong, and how to undo it, is strictly about leverage. About having enough leverage to get our full value.

It boils down to a few points:

• The share of the total national income that goes to working people has been steadily declining. That is, of the total wealth that we all create—"we all" in this case being everyone, the owners, the investors, and the workers—out of that total, the slice of the pie going to investors keeps getting bigger while the slice of the pie going to workers gets smaller. Never mind how much the pie grows or doesn't grow overall, this is about where the lines are drawn to slice it. This slipping of the workers' share is something that's been going on since World War II, is commonly accepted by both conservative and liberal economists, has been continuously documented and updated over the years, and has been officially tracked with verifiable records collected by both government and business. Details are at the end of this book.

• The loss of worker's share fell even faster after about 2001. So just to pick one point in time to focus on, we're going to consider how much difference it would make just to roll the clock back to then, to 2001 when workers were getting a little more of the pie than now.

• In 2019 the economically conservative *Wall Street Journal* calculated approximately what the money lost for workers comes to and stated, "If workers were commanding as much of domestic income as they did in 2001, they'd have...$5,100 per employed American". That is, on average, each working American should have $5,100 more per year.

• This, of course, accumulates over time. If you had $5,100 more per year on average over, say, a 35-year working career, that would be almost $180,000 total more. People who started their adult working life in 2001 are now less than 20 years into their 35-year career. They've already lost a lot, and they're going to keep on getting less than they would have, and the loss is going to keep on getting bigger, right on through to retirement. And since the slice of the pie is still shrinking, by the time they reach their later years of working, the loss is going to be even worse than $5,100 per year. The average worker earns around $45,000 per year, so a $5,100 difference would be more than a 10 percent difference. Imagine getting a 10 percent raise at the start of your working life and continuing to have that much of a difference across your 35 years. How much difference does $180,000 across those years make? Is it the college fund for the kids? Or the difference in owning your home outright when you retire versus still having a mortgage? Or, when you retire, the difference between having to stay in the same home close to where you worked versus being able to move to a nicer area where you'd like to spend retirement? Or the difference between having a stay-at-home retirement versus getting the big travel trailer and traveling all over with it? It's a big difference in your life. Oh, and note that that is per worker. So if you are a two-earner couple, double it, to about $360,000 lost.

• That is the problem. Here's a solution to consider, and let's look at what that possibility tells us. The solution would be to simply regain the negotiating power, the leverage in the employee-employer negotiations about pay, to return the way the pie is sliced back to the way it was in 2001. Never mind trying to get the pie sliced even more in working peoples' favor, like the way it was way back in 1947, or the way it was in 1970. Let's just consider the idea of rolling the clock back, the pie slicing back, just to the way it was in 2001.

Here are a few things to note about these points:

Working Peoples' Share is Declining

• It's clear that this loss of a portion of the pie is primarily about our loss of leverage, loss of power to insist on our proper share. Working people are less organized and less demanding than they used to be. Back when, if they didn't feel they were getting proper pay, they could shut an operation down to make their point. Plus we had a big recession, a big downturn in the economy in 2001, when a lot of people lost their jobs and had a hard time finding any others. That meant employers could offer less starting pay and still get people desperate for work to take it. And even after the economy recovered, employers managed to hang onto at least some of that lower rate of pay to workers. Then we had a much bigger downturn in 2008, and this time it took many years for jobs to come back. Through all that time workers were desperate and would accept lower pay. Again, as the economy recovered, pay rose some, but it's just not back to where it would have been had there never been a downturn. That is to say, companies managed to hang onto more of the business income. This smaller slice is just a matter of US having become weaker in the grand and constant negotiation between working people and powerful players. It's not like there was some necessary change in government policy or that economics just has to work this way. We just lost ground in a process of negotiation. There is no other reason for it.

• It's nothing inherent in the free market system. The market can give either result, that is, the way it is now or the way it was then, and the powerful players simply prefer the current result, that is with them getting more of the pie. And they have managed to arrange things so they get more. It's not like the way the pie was sliced in 2001, or the way it's sliced now, is more truly the free market. And it's not like changing the slicing back to the way it was would be any less of a free market. It's just that powerful players managed to find ways to finagle getting more of the pie, and they did.

• If we managed to regain our share, this has nothing to do with many of the often controversial issues that come up, like the following.

• This has nothing to do with taxing the rich more. How much the rich are taxed wouldn't need to be any different than it is now, or than it was in 2001. Maybe we do want higher taxes on the top, or maybe we don't, but it has nothing to do with this. This is just about the fact that we've been losing at negotiating, losing leverage to use in negotiating.

• This has nothing to do with redistribution. That's the term that usually goes with the idea of taxing the rich more. The idea is that the rich end up with too much of the nation's wealth and therefore we should tax some of it and use it to help middle and lower income people. In other words redistribute it. But "redistribute" has built into it its own problem. It is to "re" distribute. That must mean it was not distributed right in the first place. It's a weak position. It accepts that income is allowed to be distributed wrong in the first place, then requires taxing some of it after the fact so it can be "re" distributed correctly. A better solution is to have the leverage to get the distribution right in the first place. That is, the distribution of company income between the top and the working people. It's also better because otherwise we have to use our government programs to decide how to redistribute. Better to have proper negotiations between equals, which lets the free market sort it out. Some changes in taxes and services may or may not be needed but as an overall solution redistribution is a mistake. The more powerful and correct solution is to distribute right in the first place.

• This has nothing to do with limiting the rich. They weren't limited in 2001, and we don't need to do that now to get the pie back the way it was.

• This has nothing to do with making it so the rich just can't be all that rich. The richest in 2001 could live like royalty if they wanted to. They could do it then, and they could do that now even with the pie cut the way it was in 2001.

• This has nothing to do with harming the economy. When people talk about taxing the rich more or other similar ways to help everyone else, one argument is always that if you tax the rich more they won't be as motivated to invest, to build companies, to use their capital to create more wealth. (Actually, that's all mistaken thinking, as is covered elsewhere, but leaving that point aside for the moment.) This has nothing to do with taxing the rich more or in any way dampening what the rich do in the economy. They were doing extremely well in 2001. The economy was doing extremely well. Making the pie slices the way they were then still means that the rich and the overall economy can do great.

• This has nothing to do with anyone simply being given something. People worry that if we help people financially— by free education, or a supplement to their health care or flat-out sending checks to everyone or just boosting what we do for the poor, like more food stamps—people worry that that has

US

bad consequences. They worry that people just being given stuff creates problems. This has nothing to do with that. Maybe food stamps do need to be more or maybe less, but this has nothing to do with that. This is just about whether working people are able to get something closer to the full value of what their work is worth.

• This has nothing to do with our country being any more or less socialist or social-democratic. It has nothing to do with how much influence government has on business. It has nothing to do with social programs being more or less. We weren't a socialist country in 2001, and we don't need to be one now to achieve this goal. It's just about our having more leverage.

• This has nothing to do with right and left politics.

• This has nothing to do with the usual ups and downs of the overall economy. The typical scenario is that it's only when the economy is near the peak of one of its up and down cycles that working people finally get some benefit out of it, some easiness of finding jobs, some increase in wages. Then it's over as soon as the next downturn starts. So people who want to help working people often focus on ways to get the economy into one of those high phases. That's always going to be important, but if the pie was being sliced the way it was in 2001, it would help both in good times and bad. Good times would be even better because we'd have more of the pie, and bad times wouldn't be as bad. Of course, we want as much of the good times as possible, but this goal cuts through the up and down cycles and helps all the time.

Working Peoples' Share is Declining

• This has nothing to do with the overall wealth of the nation. There's a notion that there isn't enough money in the country for some of the things we'd like. That we can't have everyone who earns a low wage getting a big raise to a considerably higher minimum wage because businesses won't be able to afford it. There's a notion that we can't make sure everyone has healthcare because there just isn't enough money, that the nation can't afford it. This has nothing to do with those debates. It has no position on any of that. It's not about whether such ideas are right or whether they're just wishful thinking for what doesn't exist. It's not about wanting anything new. It's just about wanting to get back what we had. This is income that we know exists because we used to have it. This is just wanting the same division of slices as before, regardless how big or small the total pie really is. It's something we know exists, and it used to be in "our" pocket, and it somehow slipped into someone else's pocket, unnoticed. It's just wanting it back.

What all of this says is, it's about power. We may need higher taxes or more social programs, or not. Turning the pie slices back to what they were in 2001 may be enough or not enough. It may be a good enough goal in itself, or only part of what needs to change. But it would make a difference, a $5,100 a year per worker difference. And it has nothing to do with taxes, socialism, harming the economy, limiting the rich, or giving anything away. And that tells us something. It tells us that the single most important change is, power. That we have to have this change of regaining our power, or any other changes will just be tweaking around the edges.

Not harsh power. Not one group clubbing another group over the head kind of power. Not violent power. Leverage power. Economic power. The power to slice the pie so that we have the full value of our work, leaving the rich and powerful to have the full value of their profits on our work, but not more. The pie sliced the way it ought to be. It is the power to slice it correctly that matters. No other change, without that one, will really change anything. And if we do change that and regain our proper power, then any other changes that are properly needed will follow from that. We can sort out the exact details of taxation and social programs and other questions separately. The only thing that must be done, the only thing that matters, is regaining that leverage.

The Two Pay Systems

There are two ways that wages get set. There's the way it commonly happens now, which shortchanges US, and then there's the way it ought to be done, which gives US our full value. It's important for US to have in mind a solid picture of that second way, the way it ought to be done, because we have to be clear about what our goal is in order to make progress toward it.

The way that commonly happens now we can call the "desperation" system or the "divide and conquer" system. You are one lone person negotiating with a company, a small negotiator trying to strike a deal with a giant negotiator, or at least a negotiator bigger than you. And that bigger negotiator has all of the cards. After all, if you demand too much they'll just say, "No. Thanks for applying. Next!" Sure, sometimes employers have a hard time finding enough good workers, but the general level of what's expected for a given type of work has been set by that typical pattern of a lone applicant negotiating against a whole company which holds all the cards. For instance, the work you do might be worth $25 an hour, even after the owners get a worthwhile profit, but if they can get enough people to do it for $15 an hour, that's all that will be paid. It's a matter of how desperate people in your field have been and how low companies have typically been able to go and still get workers.

Yes, you could go to one of those websites that tracks what jobs in a given field typically pay, but that's still just telling you what people have typically settled for. It has nothing to do with what your work is worth.

The second way, the way that wages should be set, is about exactly that, what your work is worth to the company. Call it the "full value" system. To make a simple example, if one hundred workers in a widget factory make 1,000 widgets a day, and those 1,000 widgets sell for $X, then after expenses are paid (raw materials, electricity, cost of owning the building, everything else) and the owners and investors get just enough profit to make it worth doing, then the rest is what the workers are worth. Their pay should be based on that. After all, the owners got their profit, and the workers did the work, so the workers should get what their work is worth.

Of course, that's a very simplified example, and there are many other factors involved. How do we measure the value of the work of answering the phones or sweeping the floor or being the shift supervisor? But the general idea that your pay should match the value of your work can hold true. What value any job creates can be roughly determined by some research into how much profit the company makes and by knowing what different positions at different levels of skill and responsibility are worth relative to one another. Even where the exact profit of a smaller, private company can't be known, the value of similar positions in bigger public companies can be known. By that method the typical value of such work can be determined.

The final details can always be sorted out in negotiations. That's the free market at work. The free market is always the best way to sort details like which positions are worth more and how much more and which employees are worth more. Free-market negotiations are the way to sort out those details; it just has to be negotiations between a company, on the one hand, and a group of employees who have the necessary information and leverage, on the other hand. It has to be a roughly equal negotiation. It doesn't work if it's between a company who has all the cards and tiny individuals who have none.

Consider the negotiations of top-name sports players. They negotiate contracts worth seemingly absurd amounts of money. But why can they manage to do that? Because major league teams make enormous amounts of money, and a top player and their agent have a pretty good idea just how much of that enormous income is as a result of a top player. They know how much more in ticket sales and other income a team is going to make if they're winning, and they know they can be a key part of that winning, so they know what they're worth. So they demand that and they get it.

For normal workers we're not talking about getting absurd amounts. It's just that negotiation should likewise be based on your worth to the company. Your work might only be worth $15 an hour or maybe higher at $25 an hour, but if that's what you're worth, that's what you should get. If you're value to the company, after expenses and enough profit to make it worthwhile for the investors, is $25 an hour, then you should be getting that. Not $22 an hour or anything less. Just like that baseball player, if you can discover that you're worth $25 an hour, and if you have the leverage to get what you're worth, then you can get that pay.

For very small businesses, it's not practical to think of them having an employee group or having a financial analyst to study what the business is making. But that's not necessary. When all of that does get sorted out at bigger businesses, then what a particular type of job is worth will be known, and workers at smaller businesses will know what their work is worth.

Knowing what you're worth is just a matter of workers being organized enough to get some research done on it. Having the leverage is just a matter of how the laws and rules work. Politically it's difficult to get there, but technically it's straightforward.

Profits

Why should the owners get only just enough profit to make it worth doing? Why not make a killing at it? Because when the free market system is working right, then price competition should drive the price down to just enough. Companies have to keep their prices low to compete with one another, and that means they can't just slap on a huge extra profit on top. Their competitors would sell for less and undercut them and they'd go out of business. The product has to sell for enough money for the owners to make enough profit to make it worth doing, but not more than that. There are exceptions, like when a company invents something new and has exclusive sales of it or when we read about drug companies getting exclusive rights to some essential drug and charging through the roof for it, but generally speaking competition drives price down to what is a fair price.

A "fair" price has to include enough to pay workers a truly living wage though. Otherwise it means workers aren't getting paid enough and end up on food stamps and Medicaid and have no savings to cover surprise expenses and no savings for retirement. Then we end up with all of the problems of society that happen when people can't really pay their own way and can't thrive like their work should enable them to do. These are working people, mind you, not anyone looking for anything free. A fair price has to include a proper living for them or nothing else works right.

Price of goods

Won't raising wages just raise the cost of everything to the point that it costs so much more to live that you're right back where you started? No. This is because wages are just one part of the costs of making a product. Studies by economists, studies that are widely accepted, find that the price of goods does not go up nearly enough to offset the benefit of higher wages. (Links to the studies are at the end of this book.)

And remember, part of the problem is that the way the pie is sliced has been steadily shifting for decades out of the hands of wage earners. Part of what raising wages is all about is shifting the way the pie is cut back to where it used to be, more in favor of the people doing the work.

All of the wealth of this nation is created by the people who do the work. Your work is valuable. The simple rule of thumb holds true. You should get the full value of your work.

Equal Negotiators

The previous section touched on the idea of equal negotiators, but it is a key concept that needs to be at the core of our understanding of what it takes to have a country for US.

The free market is a wonderful system and everything in this book is compatible with it. This book even advocates doing things in ways that are even more faithful to free market principles than the way things are done now.

The simplest free market example is if you have some extra vegetables from your garden and your neighbor has extra firewood. The two of you negotiate what is a fair trade. If your neighbor wants too much of your vegetables in exchange for their firewood, then you move on to some other neighbor to negotiate with. When the neighbor with the firewood can't get anyone to take their over-valued deal, then they'll be forced to bring down what they want. That works both ways and works amongst all the neighbors until pretty fair trades are worked out for everyone. That same principle happens throughout the economy and generally works well.

Equal Negotiators

But then again, often it doesn't. What's wrong when it doesn't? There's a missing ingredient: rough equality.

When you and your neighbor negotiate, you are equal players. But often negotiators aren't equal. If you have to negotiate with the local hospital chain for some procedure, which it seems they want an outrageous price for, how do you negotiate with them? Likely you don't. They'll say that's the price, period. Pay it or no surgery for you.

If your neighbor with the firewood grew that into a huge lumber business, and you went offering a few vegetables for some firewood, they very well might laugh you off the property or require a much greater value in money for the wood. What used to be a perfect little trade has now completely failed. The only thing that has changed is that you are no longer equal-sized negotiators. It just doesn't work that way.

In certain circumstances a lot of small negotiators can have an effect much like one big negotiator. If one brand of canned beans raises their price much higher than other brands on the same shelf, many individual shoppers will stop buying them and the company will be forced to bring their price down. That works for beans, but it's not likely to work for you and the hospital. It's not likely to have much effect on you looking for a good job either.

But there's a way to fix that problem. In the case of that high-priced surgery, when some big insurance company negotiates with the hospital for what price it will accept for the procedure, that's two big, roughly equal negotiators, a hospital chain and an insurance company. They'll wrestle to some compromise, to some price that's truly good because it's a middle point where both sides get a fair value. That's the free market working like it should. But it only happens because they are roughly equal parties.

Wages could also be wrestled to a point that's fair to both sides, the free market working like it should, but only if employees are on equal footing with the company.

Some job applicants do hold out for higher pay and get some increase, but they still really have no idea if that's close to what their value is to the company. They just know they got more than the company's opening offer, but still no idea if that's the full value their job should bring them.

This problem of applicants not knowing what value their job would bring to the company and having no leverage anyway varies depending on how high of a position is being applied for. That is, the most valuable employees, the very highest engineers and technical innovators and programmers and high-level executives, have a better idea what their work is actually worth and more leverage to hold out for salary close to that. But the middle-level applicants are only guessing about their worth, and most of the people who actually do most of the work have no idea. It will only be an economy for US when most of US, that is, as near as possible to all of US, are actually getting our worth. And that is essential to our having an overall healthy and well-functioning country.

Everything about wages in this book is about free market negotiations, but it has to be a fair negotiation. The powerful have gradually been shifting things in their favor so that it's not a fair negotiation. What is suggested here is simply that we regain our leverage so that the dealing can be fair, and we can receive what a proper free market negotiation should get us. That only happens when negotiations are between roughly equal parties.

As it is, there are many circumstances where you have to negotiate but have no leverage. If only one mobile-phone service provider in your area has good service, you pay its price or do without. If the good internet service in your area comes through the cable TV system, you pay that price or do without. Chances are that's close to how it goes when you're looking for good work, too. Either take their offer, even if you have no idea if it's close to what your work is worth, or do without. Since that's true in many facets of life and that's true for many millions of people across the country, we are living in a country that, to a large extent, is not a free market country. It may be a free market for corporations dealing with one another, but it's not a free market for the individuals, for US. And true free market negotiations are essential to our having a country that runs for US. We have to arrange how we negotiate for wages and other things in ways that make for roughly equal negotiators, or we don't really have a free market or a country that's for US.

It's Not Just Wages. Or, What Good Will it Do if...?

Raising wages is referred to frequently in this book, but think of it as shorthand for much more than just that. It's the thousand ways that workers and consumers and citizens need to be treated with respect. It's about the other two words used a lot here, leverage and power. Leverage and power because, while we do need to be treated with respect, we cannot expect that to happen just because.

There are many good people in government and business who do treat others with respect because they are people of character, but far too often profit motives in business override respect, or the interests of the powerful override respect as they warp government. We won't get consistent respect simply out of niceness. We'll get it by using our leverage and power to require it.

We need respectful treatment across issues much broader than just wages because it does little good if all we get is decent wages. Here are just four items plucked from recent news to suggest the breadth of issues that need change. It's not the intention here to make a definitive list or a case for any particular issue, rather just to give some idea of the range of issues.

A court case found a company that worked with asbestos had no responsibility to warn workers about asbestos particles spreading from their work clothes to their family members at home, leading to cases of cancer. This was despite the company knowing the workers needed to be informed about this.

Safety guidelines for companies that deal with dangerous chemicals were relaxed despite the fact that accidents were happening nationwide at a rate of more than once every couple of weeks. These included incidents reported as "2.5 million pounds of pollutants released", "kills four workers", "emissions that cover nearby homes, cars and an elementary school playground", "Shelter-in-place orders for two elementary schools" and "explosions...evacuation of more than 70 square miles". (Details for this list are in the Notes section at the end of this book.) The official who was in charge of relaxing the rules justified it by saying that it would save industry "roughly $88 million a year". Hardly a sum worth mentioning compared to the danger involved.

A company that was "the top federal contractor in the call-center industry" had, for years, been under paying what the federal contract had required them to pay by using a simple trick. When employees were given higher levels of work, they would still be categorized as lower-level workers.

An official study of public water supplies listed many that had been contaminated by leaks from nearby chemical plants or military installations. However, the report was hidden because of the "potential public relations nightmare this is going to be".

What good does it do to have more jobs that promise good wages if the employer can get away with carelessly causing cancer, releasing toxic chemicals onto your neighborhood or schools, shortchanging the pay you're supposed to get, or contaminating the water in your home? The decades of powerful interests whittling away at things has permeated into every aspect of life and can only be corrected by a long, sustained time of working at undoing it. No single election of a favorable person or handful of changes of law or changes in policies or programs is going to correct it. It has to be a system wide regaining of our leverage and power, and then that has to have its effect over time.

In addition to wages, it's about other aspects of employment, like whether you can be denied advancement or let go for reasons of prejudice and whether issues of harassment are treated seriously and properly. It's the fine print in employment contracts that bars you from going to work for another company even for low-level jobs. It's consumer issues like the fine print that bars you from suing if wronged. It's citizen issues like whether companies near your neighborhood can carelessly release pollutants and whether policing operates the same for all people and all neighborhoods. It's whether good rules already on the books are enforced, wage-theft being a prime example of what happens when they aren't.

So, yes, wages are important, and if we have the power and leverage to get full-value wages, then we probably have the power to address these other issues, but many of these other issues must be addressed too. Wages are a good example topic and a good issue to focus on for regaining our power and leverage, but it is only if this broad range of issues are addressed that it becomes a country that is truly for US.

Is There Enough Money for US to Have More?

Isn't the idea of everyone getting noticeably better wages just wishful thinking? Isn't there simply not enough money in the economy? Or it would take extracting so much out of the rich they wouldn't want to own or run businesses anymore?

No. That kind of problem would only happen if this were about making promises about how big your paycheck should become or promises of huge handouts such as a guaranteed income. That kind of problem would only happen if this were about making promises the economy might not be able to meet. But that's not what this is about. This is only about how the money in the economy, however big or small the economy is, how that money is divided between workers and those getting business profit.

The kind of programs that give fixed promises which the economy might not be able to keep up with already exist. There already are at least some programs that might not keep up under the worst circumstances. For instance, Medicare really is a program that taxes current working-age people in order to help retired people have health care. If the number of retired people compared to the number of working-age people got to be too out of balance or a bad downturn in the economy had too many people out of work for too long, it's possible the taxes on working people couldn't keep up with senior's medical bills. (Medicare is not like a medical savings account because most people who live to old age draw more out of Medicare than they put in. The tax on working people is what really keeps it going.)

But proposals of the sort that are in this book are nothing like that. They are just about dividing the economic pie in a fair way. They're about empowering people to be able to negotiate with their employers like equals, so that a fair compromise is found which gives working people their full value while still leaving enough profit in the system to make it worth being in business. Whether the economy grows much faster than expected or shrinks because we hit a rough patch, however big or small the pie is, this is about dividing it fairly, as sorted out by free-market negotiations. Negotiations that are between equals. That is between the business owners, and the working people organized in ways that bring them up to equal leverage.

There may be other social programs that are needed, but that's not the topic of this book. Some social programs might be needed as a temporary bridge while people regain power, but then those programs might be reconsidered after power is more balanced. Some social programs that are talked about as possibilities for the future might be best considered only after power is balanced, so it can be determined at that point if there is even still a need or if the empowering of people has already solved the problem.

So no, the question of whether there's enough money is not a problem, because it's not about making promises of fixed dollar amounts.

Here are a few other side points.

• This is not about taking money from the rich in any way like taxing them more. Whether that needs to be done is a separate question but has nothing to do with what's suggested here.

• Other parts of this book describe how we are not dependent on the rich for a strong economy or thriving business. If that still sounds shocking or wrong, go back and read that section again. Even if the wealth of the wealthy was lessened some, it doesn't matter. If people having more leverage leads to the wealthy having less wealth (it's possible it will actually make them richer because an economy full of working people who are well rewarded would become a stronger, larger economy) but if it reduced their wealth at all it would not mean there's less money in the economy overall. It would just mean a little less of it is in wealthy hands and a little more is in working hands. The money would still be in the economy being spent and being saved and put into 401(k)s. Money spent ends up as profit for companies, and money saved is all in the pool of finance available for investment. So there would be no reduction in money available for doing business.

• Some of the changes that need to be made are not about money but about simple fairness, like ending wage theft or things that have nothing to do with money, like dealing seriously with harassment.

Is There Enough Money

• Some changes save money. For instance, raising typical wages, even of the lowest paid jobs, will mean fewer people qualifying for food stamps. But there are further kinds of savings. For instance, couples earning more of what their work is worth would have more options for one spouse to stay home or work part time while the kids are little, leading to the kids being in less trouble, going farther with their education, and becoming more productive adults.

• Some changes actually boost the economy. Getting more money into the hands of working people probably means they're going to spend a lot of it on things they've needed to do but have been putting off. That means business will sell more and that more goods and services will need to be produced. The overall economy will grow bigger to meet those demands.

• Regarding changing how the pie is sliced, we know from our own fairly recent past that having more going to employees worked very well and still allowed the rich to be fabulously rich.

Yes, there is room for working people to get more. You just haven't been getting your share.

Not Less Government, Not More, Correct Government

Some people get focused on the idea that anything that can be done to cut government is good. Other people get in the habit of thinking up some new government program to solve any difficult problem. Neither is going to help US achieve what we need to.

People think less government means more freedom, but that's only half right. Certainly, government can get intrusive, but if we don't govern ourselves, if we don't force our government to do its job right and create a structure in which to be free, then there is no freedom. A reduction in government does not automatically result in greater freedom. For instance, if government does not stop industry from ruining the environment we live in or financial interests are allowed to abuse how they deal with our money even more than already happens, then that is a reduction in government that results in less freedom for US. That's where the need for correct government comes in.

Correct Government

Consider that one of the things that people who want less government tend to focus on is private property. They don't want government interfering in what they can do on their private property. But if there were no laws saying uninvited people aren't allowed to trespass on their property, if there was no office of county records to document where their property lines are, and if there were no police to enforce property laws, there might as well not be private property. They could get a gun and protect their property themselves, but that just becomes a lawless land of anarchy and of domination by the most violent.

And there are things best done through government, without which we might otherwise all just be campers, each camping on our private property. Things like public education for all and the highway system. Good governance can include both the basics and things that enhance the general situation for US all.

If the "let's cut government" train gets running strong, it's just an invitation for the powerful to cut those parts of government that restrain the powerful from abusing US. Pretty much the only tool we have that's powerful enough to counter powerful interests is government, government converted to use for US. If government is minimized, it leaves US with little defense against the ways the powerful would make things work exclusively to their benefit with no regard for how that damages US.

On the other hand, focusing on government to fix problems, where the government fix is just a bandage laid on top which doesn't really fix the underlying problem, that just creates different problems.

As an example, a case could be made that food stamps are a problem, but in a way you might not expect. Food stamps are needed for the elderly and the disabled and single mothers. But food stamps for able-bodied people who are working is only a need because the economy has a lot of jobs that don't pay US a livable wage. That means companies can pay people so little they can hardly survive. The food stamp program steps in and tries to help people, but a side effect is that it makes it all the more possible for companies to pay people tiny wages because they get food stamps to help get by. It just makes the problem of ridiculously tiny wages even worse.

The underlying problem is that people don't have enough leverage to get paid what they should and, in the case of the very lowest jobs, not even enough to afford both rent and food. The food stamp program is just a way to use government to put a bandage on the problem, to cover over the problem, but this doesn't fix the underlying real problem. If the underlying problem were fixed and people could demand decent pay even for bottom-level jobs, then hardly anyone with a job would need food stamps. Then food stamps could go mostly to the others who need them, the elderly and disabled and such. For now, because there are so many under-paid jobs, food stamps for working people have to continue because simply leaving people hungry is certainly not the direction we want to go. But if we regained our power to get paid our full value, then maybe food stamps could be cut back to just those in more need. Regaining our power to get paid our full value and getting all the other changes toward a country that runs for US would solve so many problems that many of the issues there are disagreements about would largely just no longer be problems.

Focusing on just cutting government or, on the other hand, looking too much to government for patches, will not help us. Just focusing on cutting government will lead to the powerful being unrestrained and even better able to have everything work in ways that benefit them. Plus, there are government

Correct Government

programs that are a much greater help than they are a hindrance, like public education. There are some things that just won't work any other way, like it will probably take something similar to Medicare for all to finally get everyone health insurance. And there are some things that have to be done until we fix underlying problems, like continuing those food stamps for working people.

And government is an important and necessary tool in empowering US. Government could be a help to US by enforcing collective bargaining laws, so we can demand proper pay. Government could ban the fine print in employment contracts that says you can't sue if you're shorted or mistreated. It could ban similar fine print in contracts you have to sign to get services like cellular or cable or car insurance that say you can't sue them either. There are thousands of laws and rules that favor the powerful that need to be flipped to favor US. Government used by US and for US is an essential tool.

But we can't just look to government for social programs to make up for the damage done by underlying problems. Programs which leave those underlying problems unsolved. We have to focus on solving the real problems.

The goal is not minimal government, and it's not a lot of social programs. It's not about too much government or too little, it's about correct government. Government prioritizing what is most helpful to US.

That only comes from people insisting on it, and from regaining the power to mold it to work for US.

Socialism?

There's a lot of talk about socialism and about whether we should find some alternative to capitalism, and it's almost all wrong on both sides. That's unfortunate because it hides some underlying issues we really do need to consider.

First is a look at how the words socialism and capitalism are often misunderstood. Then, a look at those important underlying issues that are really what make people concerned.

There's a lot of misuse of those words because people rarely know what those words really mean. Is that even important? Yes, because it leads to two sides arguing in ways that totally miss the valid part that each side has to offer. This is kind of a nit-picking topic, focusing on the meaning of words, but it's included because it's important for understanding what's being suggested in this book and for US all to be able to debate such issues clearly. Otherwise, instead of making progress, we tie ourselves up in off-point arguments that only waste our time while we continue to slip ever lower in our place in the economy.

Anyone who simply wants more social programs, say free college or subsidized childcare, is not seeking socialism. They may not know it or say it right, but what they're suggesting would simply lead to continuing with capitalism but with some added social programs.

People who say capitalism is horrible or that it's the cause of so much of our problems are almost always just as far off base. We may consume too much, using up too much of the world's resources and creating too much pollution, we may flood ourselves with too much advertising which makes US want ever more stuff, but that's not strictly connected just to capitalism.

Real socialism means the government owns all or a great deal of private industry. Some South American countries have tried this when their government would take over a lot of private industry and finance. In the United States it is only in a very few special cases that we have government owned or controlled industries, like power utilities. They are often owned or contracted by the government because it's such an essential service that we want everyone to have it and at the lowest price possible. Other than those few cases, we don't do that here.

There is no notable push by any groups in the United States to do anything like large-scale government takeover of industry. Some of those people who don't really know what the word means say they want to be socialists or want the country to become socialist, though really they just see social programs as solutions to some problems. But their using that word scares the hell out of people who hear it and take it as meaning they want some radical change of a kind the United States has never had before. It's an unfortunate confusion of words and of ideas that sets people against one another.

The same is true of people who think we should end capitalism. They may very well wish we consumed less; they might wish everything wasn't so much about money; they might wish for a system where there isn't such a super-wealthy group who have too much power and warp everything to their advantage, leaving working people short of what they should be getting. They might want all of that, but odds are they are not against capitalism if they knew what it actually means.

For one thing, capitalism and the free market are often confused. The free market simply means you can start a business if you want, you can charge what you want, and you can operate within the economy any way you want, limited only by your resources and staying within the laws. Capitalism is another layer on top of the free market. It simply means one person investing in another. If the teenager next door is starting a lawn-mowing business and wants you to buy the lawn mower in return for a small portion of the profits, that's capitalism. You've just invested your money, for someone else to use, with the expectation you'll make a little profit in the process.

If you have some money saved up toward retirement and you want to do anything better with it than stuffing it under the mattress, if you want to put it in an interest-bearing savings account or invest it in a 401(k) plan or put a little in the stock market, that's capitalism.

So let's be clear about what most people do and don't want. Almost no one wants to end the free market. We all want to be able to work where and how we want or have a little side business. And almost no one really wants to end capitalism. We all want to hang onto our savings in some way that grows it a little bit, either by that savings account or with a little investment. Those savings and investments are good for the economy. People put their money into the bank savings accounts and then the bank lends it out to businesses that can put it to good use and grow. Almost no one wants real socialism either, as in the government taking over a lot of private industry.

Socialism?

So what is all the fuss about? Two things. Two legitimate concerns we can all understand.

One is those social programs. People advocating for them think they would help people, and in some cases they might be right. The people who feel this way would just like to see the lowest-income people and ordinary people generally get a better deal out of the economy and they think this is a way to do it. Whether you agree with social programs as the way to do it or not, we can pretty much all agree that many of the lowest-income people get a really lousy deal out of the economy, working hard and still being poor. And we can probably all agree that middle-income people, while they're not poor, are probably not getting the full value their work should bring them, and it would be good to find ways to make that right.

Some people think social programs would help these problems, and sometimes they're right. Other people are very wary of social programs, and sometime they're right too. But in both cases the general goals—the goals of the least among US not doing so poorly and the bulk of US getting a fairer deal for our work—are things we can all agree on. It's just a matter of how. And no one is really talking about ending capitalism or having real socialism. They're just using the terms wrong, and that gets the discussion all mixed up.

The second fuss is about excess: excessive consumerism, excessive concentration of wealth, excessive power and influence in the hands of a few, excessive focus on the money aspect of any issue when often it's other values that ought to be the focus (quality of life, health, evenhanded fairness to all, care of the environment, etc.). These are things we can probably all agree are problems and we would like to see improvement on them, but talk of ending capitalism or turning to real socialism just confuses the debate. Even in countries that have had real socialism it can still be the case that an upper-crust few have much more power and much more wealth and luxurious lifestyles. And it can still be the case that there's a lot of advertising which helps to drive excessive consumption.

That shows that it's really more of a human problem. It's always the case in any system, the problem of whether power accumulates in the hands of a few and whether those with that power unfairly cheat the bulk of the people. What's needed is not a radical change in what kind of system we have, but a radical change in how much it's focused on working out well for the bulk of US. We had something close to that in the New Deal era from after World War II up through the 1970s. As noted elsewhere, it primarily helped white men, but at least for a while, for that group, we showed we could have a system that focused on them doing well, and they did. We need that same kind of thing again, only this time applying it to everyone.

It's clear that oftentimes when people use the term socialism what they're really talking about is a matter of emphasis. They want a system that focuses more on the well-being of all, less on the absolute through-the-roof absurd wealth of a few, more on other values like care of the environment and fairness to all, and less on maximum wealth at the top at any cost. Use of the term socialism to signal desire for significant change toward that kind of shift in priorities is entirely understandable, and they are goals we can probably all understand. Still, use of the term has two problems. One, it makes it easy for those who want to divide US to create horror stories about socialism being the end of the things we love about America though that's not what people using the term generally mean at all. Two, it distracts from the real problem. No matter what system, we have to take hold of the power to make it work for US. As things are, the system works more for the top and only works enough for US to keep us going along with the lousy deal.

We may need more social programs. We may not. But what we do need, in any case, is a radical change in power, in the leverage of ordinary people. Once we have achieved that, then it's up to US if we want to find ways to make our economy one that consumes less or that focuses more on other values.

We need to avoid getting caught up in arguments that are off target and only get US fighting with one another while wealth and power continues to accumulate at the top. It only distracts US with arguments about radical change of the system and therefore distracts US from the truly radical change that we do need, and that is the degree to which the system focuses on working for US.

Confusion, or Exactly Where Does This Book Fit In?

It's possible that as you read this book it will seem confusing in a specific way. That is, which side is this book on? In some places it's critical of using the word socialism. It's critical of relying too much on social programs in cases where those programs are just a patch over the problem and don't get at the underlying issue. But it's open to social programs where they are best. It's open to them but takes no stand on which problems should get social programs, though a problem like healthcare, for instance, seems destined to be dealt with through a social program. It's fiercely against prejudice but it takes no stand on immigration issues. It's for radical change that would reinstate the focus on people in ways that would help everyone, including the middle-income working people in the middle of the country. But it wants the same radical change for everyone, rural and urban, of every category, and it claims that failure to have it apply to all would be failure, period. It wants to shift how much of the nation's wealth ends up with the people doing the work versus those at the top, but it's for the free market and even capitalism (as long as it works to the benefit of the people). It even wants to use the free market as the tool with which to shift income more in favor of the working people. That last part may seem head-spinningly contrary since free market advocates are usually trying to help investors, not workers.

Is this book taking a stand in the middle just to be in the middle, as some politicians do? No. The middle can be correct sometimes, but often it's just where it's safe and nothing much happens. This book is for radical change in specific ways.

Some people go to great lengths to take an unusual mix of positions just so they won't fit into any typical category. They might care more about pride in their independent positions than in whether their positions make sense taken together. Is that what this is? Just intentionally trying not to fit any pigeon hole? No. If you consider the rest of the book, there is a consistent thought line that runs through it.

The fact that it might strike US as confusing is a red flag that we've become locked into set ways of thinking. Those ways may not be doing US the most good. We've been gradually herded into a few typical positions.

Sometimes we've been herded in one direction by those who have something to gain. Either they can stir US up to become their big audience, which makes them rich and famous, or we become their supporters and voters. Other times we've been herded by people with the best of intentions who really feel for those in need, whether they're trying to help the least fortunate or trying to help average people who aren't getting what they should. They feel for them but can't envision a solution big enough to really solve things, so they push little fixes that would help a little. But those little fixes just end up being part of the pile of bandages on top of bandages that never really fix the underlying gaping wound.

We've also been herded by groups who take up the banner of their being our champions and who get themselves elected, but then they are so timid about it that things just get worse. That in turn leads to our being herded by leaders and groups who are the more violent or destructive or bigoted or self-centered, who prey on those of US who are frustrated, and they manage to gain ground because of the vacuum of progress.

We end up herded into one of a couple of typical paths. Some get on a self-centered course of thinking we need to make the entire system run of, by, and for just people like ourselves and drive everyone else out or push them down. They think that's the way they can get theirs. The other path is thinking of ourselves as almost powerless except for the ability to harass the government into fixing things for US. The government should fix many things, but not by just piling on more bandages.

Both of the standard options are weak positions. Positions we have chosen over time out of being desperate for some approach that will make things better. But the proper solution is bigger and deeper and more radical, so much so that it's hard to imagine. That it is hard to imagine is part of the reason we've gotten herded into these lesser positions. Leaders and media and our own thinking have a hard time picturing the larger solution or imagining that it could actually happen, and so we end up with these lesser positions that only allow things to continue to slip ever worse.

The proper solution doesn't feel like it fits into any of the common pigeon holes. It doesn't fit because it's large enough to do well by all of US and doesn't need to be limited to just helping people like ourselves. And it's large enough that it gets rid of the need for many of the government bandages. So, if reading about this doesn't fit with our pigeon holes then you might end up scratching your head and wondering, where does this fit in?

If you've been focused on just helping people like yourself, then time to broaden your thinking, because the only solution that will really help you is one big enough to help everyone, even those you think of as "others". On the other hand, if you've gotten so used to assuming that any position that doesn't support this or that social program can't truly be interested in what's best for people, then time to broaden your thinking too. Consider that the very ideas for those programs you want are just the result of our underpowered position and the underpowered ideas we grab hold of for little improvements.

This is not about being different for the sake of being contrary. It's not about middle ground. And yet the radical change proposed isn't anything contrary to American experience either. It's change that's bigger than we have allowed ourselves to think but in ways that we already know how to do from past American experience (which we can improve on). It's about change that's big enough that it ends the need for the pigeon holes we've created and would result in all of US better off than anything that ever came out of any pigeon-hole idea. Confusing? That might be good. That might mean your head is letting go of more limited ideas and taking steps toward looking at a bigger picture than we've considered. A bigger picture that would do very well for all of US.

But the Robots are Coming. What then?

Is the advancement of automation really so important it needs its own chapter? Yes, for two reasons. One, because while the effects of automation are always important, they're going to have a much larger effect on US going forward. Two, our attitude toward it gets to the heart of the change that needs to happen. Change that needs to happen in our own heads.

That the country needs to be running for the benefit of US becomes even more important if we consider the effects that robots and automation are already having. Effects which will be booming in the coming years. It's important because automation is going to be either hurting US or helping US. There is no middle ground. Which comes to pass largely depends on whether we have the leverage to hold onto the full value of our work.

It's not as if, if we don't get more leverage, we'll be just the same as now, no better or worse off. No. If we don't gain more leverage, then robotics, automation, and artificial intelligence will hurt us. Standing still means we'll end up worse off. On the other hand, if we have the power to get our full value, then the benefits of automation will be helpful to working people, and we will be even better off.

Automation, and pretty much any advance in technology, does help the overall country in the long run, and eventually everyone ends up at least a little better off. But, of course, in the short run technology often affects jobs. As the cell phone replaced the land line it displaced people who ran phone lines. Automation in factories eliminates jobs directly.

Economists say that even when technology eliminates jobs in the short run, it eventually enriches us all. For instance, cars eliminated the jobs that had to do with horses and buggies but, because we could all get around faster and haul more goods farther in trucks, ultimately the nation was enriched. The economists are right, in the long run.

But when someone is in the middle of their work life and their job disappears or, worse, a whole town goes down the drain because the plant the town depended on is gone, then someone who is middle-aged has to start over in a new field and maybe move their whole family. They may get another job, but they may never catch up to where they were on pay. Maybe their kids will be better off because the nation will be richer in the future, but that's not much help to the person out of work.

And robotics and artificial intelligence may be even more disruptive than other changes in technology. Rather than just shifting work, as from buggies to cars, it might make a much bigger difference in the amount of work needed than did other technological changes of the past. That's because, in order to produce the number of goods and services that people buy, employers may not need to hire all that many people. There might be a lot of people simply not needed for work. Or the typical number of hours an employee gets might become less, so they have a job, but it's not enough hours.

That's a double-edged problem because not only is that bad for the people who don't get work, it also means they can't buy the things they normally would. That means businesses sell less, the whole economy becomes less, and even the rich end up with less because the businesses they own are selling less. That, in turn, means businesses hire still fewer, so yet more people don't have work as a result.

To some extent this is self-correcting. Products made by robots can be made cheaper, so they'll probably sell for less. (If patterns hold, though, that will be only partly true, and businesses will manage to hang onto some of the extra, and the rich will get richer, and the way the pie is sliced will go even more to the top.) So it will self-correct some, but not enough to make it all right, and all of those without work will still be in dire straits.

What should happen, if the benefits of automation were shared by all, is that as a factory needs fewer employees, that is, where, say, it used to take one hundred employees working the assembly line and now it only takes ten to mind the robots, the pay for those remaining ten should go up.

Think of it this way. If a factory used to make 1,000 things a day, big screen displays or power drills or whatever, that means that each of those one hundred employees was producing 10 products a day. The pay for each employee should be equal to the income on sales of those 10 products, minus all expenses and minus a reasonable profit for the investors. With automation and the factory now only needing ten employees to produce the same 1,000 products, each employee is now producing not just 10, but 100 products per day. The pay should still be calculated the same way: the income on those products, now 100 products per employee, minus expenses and reasonable profit. So the pay should go up proportionately.

So the pay should go up ten times what it was? No, not ten times, as explained next, but it should go up just as much as the profits for the owners go up. They should all benefit roughly equally from the new efficiency.

The pay may not go up as much as it appears at first because, while the number of employees went from one hundred down to ten, the expenses went up, to buy and maintain the robots. So it's not an exact trade off, but certainly the automation will be cost effective. That's why manufacturers will continue to rush into using automation as much as possible, because they find it profitable.

Also the selling price of the products will go down. If one company automates, then so will their competitors. They'll all be making the products cheaper, so they'll compete on cutting prices and the price will go down. That's a benefit to consumers. Consumers can, and generally do, benefit from automation too.

But the price won't go down so much that it wipes out all of the added profit. The typical pattern seems to be that automation both reduces the price of products some and increases the profit of the business. Why else would a business bother to automate if it wasn't going to get something out of it?

The question is, does the extra profit, that portion that the company hangs onto, does that all go to the top? Or does it get shared properly with the workers? If automation cuts a lot of jobs or eliminates a lot of the hours needed to make things, then the pay of the workers needs to go up, a lot. It's the only way the economy keeps on working right, as is explained next.

So does the pay going up a lot like that seem to be too much? Won't those ten employees be getting some very big paychecks? Well, here are two ways of looking at it. Take your pick.

With the pay going up a lot, then the expectation would be that people could afford to work fewer hours. Maybe what we typically think of as a full-time job becomes only twenty hours a week. In fact, we would hope that it works out that way so that everyone who needs to work gets enough hours, say those twenty hours it takes to earn a living, rather than a few people getting forty hours and huge paychecks while a whole lot of others have no work at all.

Pay going up a lot could also mean many more parents who choose to be couples would be able to go back to the days of one parent being able to stay home during the child-rearing years. That doesn't need to mean women returning to the oppression of being housewives when they don't want to be. A husband could be the stay-at-home parent too. But it means having the income to have the option of one staying home, and it means a lot of kids having parents who have the option to do more parenting if they want. The side point here is not just about parenting, but how automation should improve our lives. All of our lives, not just the top.

People being able to work less is the whole point of automation, if properly applied. In the future, when automation is applied everywhere that it can be, no one will be doing grunt work. People who want to be creative will still work at developing new products and such, but no one will work an assembly line, drive a truck, answer phones, wait tables. There will still be jobs that can't be automated or ones where we prefer human interaction, and there will be jobs minding the robots, but the total number of human hours needed might be much less. If such a world is done right, everyone still needs to get their share of working hours to earn a living. However, with less overall work needed, they have to be able to earn that living with fewer hours, or maybe fewer years. That is, they would need a level of pay that would allow for a shorter work life but still enable them to save up for a long retirement. In any case, it means that pay per hour has to go up to meet that need.

The alternative is, of those one hundred employees in our imaginary factory, ten would get retrained to mind the robots. Maybe they'd get a little more pay because it's a job that takes a little more skill. The other ninety simply become unemployed with no recovery, possibly becoming homeless, barely subsisting on whatever the food banks and charities offer, and definitely not contributing to the well-being of society the way they'd like to. Of course, there's always crime as an option. It's a bad option, but if you make a lot of people desperate, a certain amount will turn to crime.

A variation on how to deal with this is that we have some big, national, guaranteed income, so those ninety get, say, barely enough to not be homeless. But there's no dignity in that, and no guarantee the next round of elections won't lead to cuts in the guaranteed income. And people living on government payments are not likely to have much political power, so whether the government's support continues at all would be uncertain.

Ironically, these ninety people having little or no income would even be bad for the powerful interests, the owners and investors, because it means those who are out of work have no money to spend on products, so businesses will sell less.

But don't worry about the owners. With robots making things and only ten employees to mind them, business will be profitable. Price competition will drive prices down somewhat, but somehow most of the major companies in most of the major industries keep making more, and their slice of the pie keeps getting bigger.

So the huge increase in automation that is to come can either result in everyone having an easier life, or result in a whole lot of people effectively cut out of the economy, clinging to the edges, clinging to bare survival and all of the rotting of society that goes with that.

After all, someone is going to get the benefits of automation. Why should it go more to the investors than to US? It is our innovation and our work that has led to automation. Why should it be allowed to end in a bad result? We should get our full value for our work, and we should get our full share of the benefits of automation.

Getting to the good result, the easier life for all of us, will take a monumental struggle of leverage. Leverage to demand and get our proper share of it, based on the value of the work that we all do which makes it all go. Automation is going to change things. Standing still in terms of leverage will mean losing ground in terms of results. Making the economy what it ought to be—of, by, and for US—is the only way to avoid the future being even more of the opposite—of, by, and for powerful interests. But, hey, we're US. Numerous and strong. We can do this. We just have to actually, you know, do this.

Our reaction

As noted at the start of this chapter, this subject gets to the heart of what needs to change, and that change is in our own minds. When the effects that automation will have on jobs are discussed, it often leads to worries of lost jobs. We end up with a negative reaction to news of automation, which is a crazy and backward state of mind.

Automation by definition means a reduction in effort needed. Anything that reduces the effort needed for US all to live our lives should be joyous news. If it's a kitchen appliance that's going to make kitchen work even quicker and easier, that seems like a great idea. But if it's automation that affects our job, we have the opposite reaction. The thought is, "Oh, no! Fewer hours! More layoffs!" We get stressed and worried. And why do we react that way? Because it is so deeply ingrained in our minds that anything that could possibly be used to benefit business at our expense, will. That this is just the way things work and the automatic result and it never even crosses our minds to expect otherwise. When, actually, anything that automates, that is anything which reduces the work it takes to run our nation, again, should be joyous news. Even if we're just acknowledging the fact that, as things are, it's likely to only help the top, our thought should be to be incensed and outraged that an advancement in human technology should go only to the benefit of the top and be a detriment to the rest of US in lost wages. Even if someday we'll all be better off for the innovation, the fact that the near-term gain should all go to the top and hurt US is something we should be outraged to be confronted with.

That this is the typical scenario is an indication that radical change is needed, but first a radical change has to happen inside each of our heads. If we haven't changed our outlook so that we have a deeply ingrained automatic reaction to look at things with the assumption that it should all work to the benefit of US, then we haven't had that radical change in our own heads. If we ever find ourselves reacting in ways that are sensible, like hearing that automation hurt some workers and automatically thinking, "What? It hurt workers not helped them? Why didn't those workers get their full share of the benefit of automation?" then we know our head has changed.

That change, in our heads, is really the only change that matters. It is that change that will help US realize just how much power we already have and start to use it. If enough people have that change in understanding, then change will happen, relentlessly, possibly slowly, but surely, gradually over time yielding to the pressure of our insistence on our being given our full value, both in work and in how we want this country run.

Radical change has to happen, and it has to happen in your head.

Wage Theft is Like a Thermometer

Wage theft is a problem in itself, but it's also an indicator of our loss of power. The fact that there is virtually no enforcement is a measure of just how far our position in the priority of things has fallen.

It can also be an indicator of how we, that is the rest of US, how united we are. That's why this issue has it's own section. It's an indicator of whether we really want to be united as US or whether we'd rather just go along as is, as is described further down.

Size and scope

Wage theft is a much bigger problem than most people are aware and reaches to much higher job levels than most think. It results in many billions of dollars of lost wages in the country each year. (References are in the notes at the end of this book.) It affects low-level jobs but also much better jobs. Some very big businesses that are usually considered to be places for good white-collar jobs have paid out hundreds of millions of dollars in court settlements for shorting workers' pay. That's right, many of the companies thought to offer many of the best jobs have had to pay, not just millions, but hundreds of millions in fines, and that's just the cases that were successfully brought and settled. Many top name high-tech companies, the biggest banks, the top parcel delivery services, insurance companies, and others have paid many tens of millions. Each. For some companies it's up into the hundreds of millions. Worse, it's safe to assume that those settlements were a comprise and that the employees actually lost much more than that.

There are many ways employers can steal from you. From the crude, for instance, just shorting the paycheck or paying less than minimum wage or bullying employees into working extra hours off the clock, to the more subtle. If you're a skilled tech worker, you should be able to sell your skills to the highest bidder, but a bunch of high-tech companies agreed not to hire each other's workers, effectively blocking you from finding your highest pay. Companies that fill government contracts are sometimes required by those contracts to pay certain wages for certain job levels, but the employer can simply require you to do the higher-skilled work but keep you labeled as being in a lower-skilled category.

For the most part there is zero enforcement of wage theft. When there are a lot of employees losing a lot of money in a single company, then it can be enough to be worthwhile for a legal team to pursue it, which is how some of those big settlements came about. But if you're, say, a thirty-five-year-old single mom raising your kids on what you make waitressing at a nice restaurant, but they require you to spend an hour before your shift, off the clock, preparing salads, or they refuse to pay the extra that should come with overtime hours, and you want to get some help to get what's coming to you? Good luck.

It varies by state, but typically help is either hard to find or nonexistent. The police would just tell you that even though someone has stolen what's yours, you have to find help through regulators or courts or anything but them. If the employer steals that same cash out of your wallet, call the police. But if they steal it out of your paycheck, police want nothing to do with it. Is there a labor enforcement regulator? In some states there literally is none. In that case your problem has to rise to a much higher level to trigger federal enforcement into action, and if it's less than that, there is no government body that cares. In states where there is some labor department, it's often a sub-department under the corporate department whose main focus is promoting business growth, not helping workers.

You can take your case to small claims court but only to claim very small amounts, and you have to know what you're doing, and there's no one to enforce payment even if you win. If it's more than that, it goes to civil court, which means it has to be big enough for lawyers to feel they can get your money back plus enough for their fees, which isn't likely. So you're not likely to find a lawyer who will take it on a pay-if-you-win contingency arrangement.

So for many people in many situations the reality is that you did the work, you had your wages stolen, and there ain't nothin' you can do about it.

What compounds it is that even if you win, nobody cares. If an employee wins a civil court case for stolen wages, it's very likely the employer is stealing from others. Maybe the employer just didn't like that one employee, but it's much more likely that employer is stealing just as much from as many as possible. But there is no agency that is likely to take note of that and follow up. Other kinds of crimes do get follow up. If the police learned that some store was slipping counterfeit money in with the good when giving change or some restaurant was finding a way to trick the credit card machine into charging more than what it shows or some convenience store was selling drugs under the counter, they'd recognize that for what it is, a crime, and be all over investigating them for the proof that it's a pattern of their business and shut it down. But if an individual employee wins a case against wage theft, no one notices, and the employer can just keep right on stealing from the rest.

There is perhaps no clearer indicator that the government officials we have elected, and the decisions we have allowed them to implement are not properly focused on achieving our best interests the way they are supposed to.

There isn't much in our national philosophy that's more sacred than work. Yet to an amazingly common degree, and a hugely expensive degree, people simply don't get paid for work they did. Yet despite that huge problem there is so little effort put into dealing with it that it remains huge and expensive. What clearer indication could there be that what is important to US is not important in the way things are run.

Powerful interests have warped the focus into being on other priorities. A re-creation of the proper balance of power needs to happen.

But what if wage theft doesn't affect you?

The issue of wage theft is also a test of you, the reader. You may be a white, middle-income person or at least financially secure enough that wage theft seems unlikely to affect you and yours. You may imagine that it only happens to undocumented workers or workers in very low-wage and low-status jobs, like kitchen help, landscape workers, food delivery people, and low-end temp jobs. You might think the only time it happens to anyone in your world is if it's kids who are high-school students at their first fast-food job. You'd be wrong, but that's not the point. The point is, does this seem like something that doesn't affect your world and therefore is not important to you?

Of the issues described in this book, are you mostly focused on getting better wages for middle-income people, while if the lowest-income people in the lowest-status jobs continue as is with little improvement that just doesn't seem like much of a problem? Then look at your priorities carefully because you are looking at the problem. What happens to the lowest-status members of US, what happens to the ones furthest removed from you, who seem to have the least to do with your world, what happens to them is like a mirror. You're looking at a mirror, and in it you see the problem.

The way that we lost our leverage has, yes, a lot to do with powerful interests warping things and, yes, a lot to do with those politicians who have claimed to be for the little guy but then have been wimps about fighting for US, but it also has to do with US. When white people aren't just as concerned about minority people gaining improvements too, when middle-income people aren't just as concerned about the lowest getting a much better and fairer deal too, then we are not united. And a united front is the only significant power we have. If we're mostly concerned about improvements for people like ourselves and not so committed to demanding as much change for others, then we are not US. And without the power of US, there will be no change for US.

Have a clear image in your mind that US is all of US, or don't bother hoping for change.

The Fix, the What

Just exactly what change is being suggested in this book? And how would that come about? The "how" follows in the next section, though it's worth noting that how has nothing to do with violence or anything illegal (well, maybe some civil disobedience demonstrations, but nothing more serious.) This section is a description of the "what".

The change needed has been referred to in previous chapters as a need for power, for the people to have the power, the leverage, to get a good deal. Talking in terms of the people and power may sound dangerous or radical, but it's not. We have had examples of the people having more power in our not-so-distant past, and that came about by methods that were in keeping with American ways.

In previous chapters there have also been many references to wages, to people having the leverage to be able to negotiate and get a good deal on wages, but the issue of wages, as noted, is just a sort of shorthand for much broader general power that we need for a whole set of issues beyond just wages. Power to be treated well as customers, to make the government effective for us on issues like unsafe products and pollution, to maintain rights like not having our privacy casually compromised by either government or business, to ensure fully equal treatment for all groups.

That variety of issues is listed to point out that it all goes hand in hand. If we don't have the power to, for instance, force proper treatment by big corporations, or to have laws generally not stacked against US, then we won't have the power to get correct wages or proper results on any of the issues. On the other hand, if we do have the power, then we will want to apply it to every issue that is important to US. It's something of an "all or nothing" situation. We will either have the proper power or we won't. If we do, then we would naturally apply it to everything.

So what form would those changes take? What are some of the steps and outcomes that would happen? Below is a sample list, but the process would involve finding many of the laws and regulations at every level, in federal government and in state and even local governments, finding the ones that are tilted against the best interests of ordinary people and tilting them back the other way. It has taken powerful interests many decades of having undue influence to gradually warp the entire system and create laws and ways of doing things that work against US and for them. It will take an equally thorough process to undo all of that, and for some things it may take a long time. It takes gaining power and hanging onto it so that that long process can gradually influence everything about how our nation and our economy operate.

Sample list

• Any policy that makes workers more valuable and leads to their better pay and benefits and treatment. For instance, letting the unemployment rate get lower before the Federal Reserve dampens the economy (by raising interest rates). Without going into detail, the policies of the Fed, during good economic times, can cause the benefits to workers to stop short, or not be as good as they could. Fed policies could be adjusted in favor of workers.

• A serious war on wage theft, which is a problem that is shockingly common.

• Ending the forcing of new hires to sign a form saying they won't sue their employer if the employer does something that they ought to be sued for. That little detail in the course of signing onto a new job is pervasively common.

• Some items that have nothing to do with employment but with how we are treated as customers. For instance, many nursing homes have a contract clause that says if the nursing home either gives you a bad deal or mistreats your granny, you can't sue. End having any such clause.

• Companies that repeatedly rip off their customers, despite repeatedly being caught at it, at some point cross a line where it's clear they never will be a fair company. They should be forced to sell the company to new owners and any proceeds go to restitution first.

"Cancel culture"

Would a push for change just turn into a lot of what have been referred to as "cancel culture" events? That is, when a celebrity or business does something offensive, like the owner is accused of sexual assault or a celebrity says something prejudiced, then public reaction leads to them being "canceled". They lose their media position or the business is boycotted. No doubt some of that will happen because sometimes it's deserved when public people do stupid things, but also because as we begin change it's bound to be somewhat messy. But as things shift to being more on behalf of people then there will be less need for such canceling events. If women were listened to about harassment in the first place and could get such incidents dealt with at the time, or if prejudice was much less tolerated, then there would be less chance for a habit of it to build up in a business over time, and then there would be no need for it to erupt later in some big reaction to a long pattern of past wrongs. And as things are run more for US, over time we will develop good systems for dealing with such problems in ways that are proper and fitting for both the accuser and the accused. These eruptions of cancel culture events are a symptom of our having little power and only being able to get justice in fits and starts. When things are running on our behalf in the first place, there will be less need for such events.

A labor share policy

Here's one policy that could help and gives a solid measurement with which to gage our progress. Enforce improvement in the labor share. The labor share is the way the pie is sliced, how much of company income goes to workers. It's the measure that has been slipping for decades, as described in a previous chapter.

The labor share should be tracked and adjusted much like we do with inflation. With inflation we go to great lengths to try to accurately measure what the current rate is. There are a lot of solid economic numbers, like the cost of goods at the grocery store and the way certain business trends are going, that give us very solid grounds to know how inflation is doing. Having measured it, then we go to great lengths to adjust it. We don't force it, like, say, forcing businesses to raise or lower their prices, but we do all sorts of things to create pressure in the market to make it tend to go more up or down as needed. The Federal Reserve raises or lowers interest rates, buys or sells bonds, and takes other measures, all to try to keep the economy in healthy shape on the understanding that a right rate of inflation is a key element of that. The inflation rate is so important that many of our laws and regulations reference it.

The problem with measurements like inflation and GDP (Gross Domestic Product) are that they don't tell us how the average worker is doing. You can have a booming economy with rapidly growing GDP, but the average worker might still not be doing so well. We need a measurement that gets closer to the ground, closer to indicating how working people are doing. The labor share is a good candidate for that.

In order to measure the labor share there are solid economic numbers we can work with. Having measured it, then, as with inflation, we should go to great lengths to push it toward its optimal value. We shouldn't force it by, for instance, forcing wages to go up or down (other than the minimum wage, which is needed to keep people from being paid intolerably low wages), but we can create pressure in the market to make it tend to move in the desired direction. If the labor share has room to get bigger, closer to what it was in, say, the 1960s, then increasing workers' ability to have collective bargaining could help. During recessions, having a jobs program to keep people working could help. That helps the labor share because the more people who are working, the harder it is for employers to hire, and they have to offer more. To keep an eye on when the labor share should stop being pushed up, a good measure is when inflation is threatening to get carried away, not just a little on the high side, but actually looking like an inflation spiral.

Labor share ought to be seen as just as essential of a measurement as inflation, and efforts to optimize it ought to be just as key as are our efforts toward proper inflation. It ought to be central to our economic laws and policies.

Wages are not all that's important. As previously noted, we also need power to change how we are treated as consumers and as citizens. But labor share has the advantage of being a measurable quantity that we can use to direct policies to move in the right direction.

Gray changes and black and white changes

Some changes that could be made are in a gray area of whether they're the right changes. Should we change corporate laws to require more employee representation on corporate boards? Should we change policies to encourage more worker-owned co-op businesses, or would that hurt business efficiency? We should seriously consider any such ideas that seem good and, in some cases, just go ahead and experiment and see what helps.

But many changes, like those in the sample list section above, are clear items where there is something working against individuals and favoring bigger interests and it should be changed. There's a great deal of improvement that could be made quickly on those kinds of items. Change that could happen just as quickly as they can be taken hold of and the decision made to change them. The speed of that is entirely a matter of our degree of leverage.

More details

A long list of the details of the "what" that needs to be changed is no doubt already in the minds of many people who work in agencies and organizations. Those who can see the many ways things work against people, and who would love to change them if they had the chance. Just as it is many of US who actually make the biggest corporations succeed, likewise, it is many of US who run the agencies and organizations and know where the changes are needed. And they are capable of making them happen.

Go to any agency of government that affects working people, like agencies affecting policy on work, or on international trade and jobs going overseas, or on justice and law and whether law is applied to all groups equally, and whether justice is applied to bankers the same as others. Go to any such agency, find someone who is high enough up that they have a good handle on how the agency works, who would seriously like to see the agency do right by regular people, and we could pick their brain all day long about what needs to change. They would have an endless list of laws and rules and standard ways the agency operates that tend to favor the powerful, laws and rules and ways that need to be flipped to favor people. The same could be done to get a list for any level of government, as well as for corporate policies.

US and the what

If what is suggested here as steps to fix what's wrong is still vague, it's because the fix involves so many changes in so many areas of life. It is precisely because the fix requires so many

115

little fixes that it seems vague. It is precisely because the way that happens is by such a fundamental shift in power that it's hard to boil it down to just a handful of key policies that need to change. But, as with every aspect of this, it's all about US. We're the ones who know where the problems are. We're the ones who know what the fixes are. We're the ones who are very capable of getting things running right. We just have to make it happen, and that gets to the question of the next chapter, the "how".

How

The how is in three parts. One is grassroots, bottom-up action. Action that we all participate in to drive policies and laws, to organize as employees and as citizens, and to drive change at all levels.

A second part is top-down. We need that pincer movement of pressure from both the bottom and top. From the bottom to give bold leaders the support to make changes and from the top to actually take those steps and enact the laws and policies. There have been times when good leaders led change, but their actions were almost always made possible by people pushing from below. In fact, sometimes it is the pressure from below that is the real story. President Richard Nixon, from his record before being president and his political stances, would probably not have been expected to drive important changes focused on people and their priorities. But there was pressure from the bottom up, and he, probably with the intention of winning votes, enacted the EPA that tries to protect the environment, the Equal Employment Act that tries to ban discrimination in hiring, the OSHA agency that tries to make workplaces safe, and other similar policies.

How

The third part is a matter of our understanding. If we act collectively and insistently, we can make all of these changes. We're just constantly in the mode of thinking we can't. The only reason a small minority of powerful interests can warp things to their advantage is because we let them. Because we think we can't get our interests to be first.

It's also, understandably, because we're busy earning a living and trying to keep our lives together. But it's not even as if this is a contest that we can try and it might or might not succeed. If we all put in our part of being involved in the change, if we act together and are unrelentingly insistent, there is no change we cannot compel. The power of 330 million people cannot be resisted. And not just any 330 million, but the very ones they count on to be their consumers and customers. The very ones who are their employees and do all the work that makes their investments go. The very ones they need votes from.

Of course, there will be plenty of US who don't get involved, and we will have things we disagree on. But if enough of us are active and if we have enough overlapping interests to at least agree on a general thrust of a country focused on being for US, then, yes, we would be an undeniable force for the change we want.

And success will bring more people in. When some, who don't get involved early on, see progress that surprises them, which looks like real change that helps them, they'll want to get on board too, and it would tend to snowball.

To give you some idea of the boldness and confidence we should act with, if we can't find leaders who will do the top-down part as we need, then we should make our own. We don't need to just count on luck to bring us another Franklin Roosevelt, who led the New Deal era that's been referred to in this book. Instead, there are plenty among US who are capable of high office, and they wouldn't be alone. It would be some of US who would be their competent staff supporting them. We can raise leaders from among US.

And, yes, powerful interests have money, but so do we, if we just put it to collective use. Note Bernie Sanders, who came close to becoming the presidential nominee, twice, while refusing to take anything but small donations of those who supported him. Regardless of your politics, he proved it could be done.

If you doubt either the idea that popular insistence works or the idea of leaders coming from among US, just look at recent history. In the 1970s it rather quickly became a popular position among many, that is, among the US of the time, that we needed to take care of our environment, which we had been doing almost none of. Of course, others had been trying to get that message across long before that, but the point is that once it became a popular opinion among so many people, it wasn't long before there were laws on the books and programs in place taking big steps on that issue. The same thing on the 1960s push for full legal civil rights, even if that still left a long way to go on prejudice. The same with ending the Vietnam War. The same with the acceptance of gay marriage. The same with the recent greater awareness of the constant prejudice in policing and other ways, which black people deal with constantly.

Various factors play a part in any issue finally coming to a point of change. But regardless of how you felt about any of those issues at the time, the point is, when enough people changed their minds and when enough people insisted some issue had to change, then change happened. When, for whatever the reason at the moment may be, we finally realize some change is needed or finally won't accept waiting anymore, very quickly big changes happen. Why? Because that's the power we have. We just rarely flex that muscle and get what we need in order for the country to be for US.

Look at some of the leaders who have either stepped up from the ranks or been pulled to the top by US. Just recently we have had young women of color with no political background decide the heck with waiting for change, they'd do it themselves, and ran for Congress and won. Whether you like their positions or not, there's no denying they did it. People are very split about the election in 2016 but there's no denying there was a big grassroots expression of, "we don't want the same old, we want change" that was a part of it. The same happened with Senator Bernie Sanders, who was the kind of candidate you would expect to be an also-ran, merely trying to get a little attention to his causes, because he didn't come across like a typical candidate or take the typical stances. But there were so many of US who wanted what he was saying to be heard that we pulled him up from the minor league to almost winning his party, twice. Like his ideas or not, the rise of his campaign is a story of the power of US.

Look a little deeper at just how much those recent changes say about our power. Look at the way a greater awareness of how black people endure prejudice created a sudden flurry of changes. Changes in business policies, in laws, in policing policies, in long-ingrained offensive pieces of anti-black culture, like the Mississippi flag, which after more than one hundred years was suddenly seen as a problem and changed, by the state leadership themselves, in a matter of weeks. Why? Because suddenly enough people made it clear these things had to change, and they did. There's a lot more to do on the issue of prejudice, but it was an impressive flurry of changes.

US

A similar cascade happened not long before when women's complaints of harassment and assault, which they had been trying to get taken more seriously as long as anyone can remember, suddenly were taken more seriously and steps were taken. Why? Because enough people made it clear it had to change.

And consider, as noted, the recent crop of new leaders popping up out of the grassroots. There's plenty of reason to think that many people are getting some idea of their power to bring change. Plus, we did something similar almost a century ago with our demanding a New Deal and our installing a president who would make it happen. It might seem like it would be surprising to have the awareness of our power take another big step up, and have that bring about big changes on our behalf, but if you look at what we've done recently and what we've done in the past, then, far from being unrealistic or surprising, it is clear. That kind of big step is neither an unreachable stretch nor unheard of. It's just a matter of whether we chose to do so.

So if you're wondering what magical solution this book could offer, there is no magic, because it's not up to anything in this book. To look someplace where you can see the solution, look in the mirror. Anytime you and the rest of US want change and realize we can have change, it's ours to be had by insisting on it.

That and the follow-up work to carry it through. But we're good at that. At work.

How to start? With whatever steps you can find close at hand and then get better at it as you go. Join local grassroots groups working on any kind of improvement for US. Support good candidates. Run for office. Help start new grassroots groups where new ones are needed. We're clever. We're capable. Most importantly, we've done it before.

And exactly what change should it be? Again, look in the mirror. What change do we want? As noted, we have had change in the past. After the Great Depression and the hard times of the 1930s there was a lot of pressure from the bottom up for the country to be run more for US. And it was those same people who pulled into power a leader, Franklin Roosevelt, who would work that way from the top down, and they gave him the support he needed to make a lot of change. It wasn't so much a dramatic change in the system as it was a dramatic change in how much the system ran for the benefit of US. It wasn't a perfect era, but it shows what we can do.

The choice is ours because, really, the country already is of US, by US, and even for US. It is for whatever we have chosen. We have chosen to allow powerful interests to have much of their way. It's a choice we've made by mistake, from not understanding that it didn't have to be that way; but, in any case, the country is the way it is today because that's what we have chosen and allowed. The question is, is it the way we want? If we chose to be unified enough and insistent enough, it will become whatever we choose. It's not even a matter of it might. If there's enough of US and we have some common general goals we are unified enough on, then it's not that it might change according to what we choose. It will change. It can't help but change.

There are three things that generally stop people from having their choice. One is being unaware that they have the power, which has been our problem and which we could change. Another is being in a country where violent authoritarians mow down their opposition, as did Joseph Stalin and Mao Zedong, and China in Tiananmen Square.

Fortunately, we have much more freedom. The third is powerful interests using propaganda and lies to divide US. That's also something that's our choice, whether we allow that to succeed.

Every elected official is chosen by US. Every office of an elected official is run by US, and their policies carried out by US. Every aspect of how the country runs is either chosen by US or allowed by US. If the country favors powerful interests, that's on US. On the other hand, if it favors our interests, that's US running the country for US. And that is the ultimate statement about US. Yes, the country needs to change to favor US, but don't read that as "Someone has allowed the country to be warped in ways that put US second" or "Someone needs to be made to change the priorities back to US".

Someone has let things slip and could set things right, but who should we get mad at about it? Who should we focus on who needs to be pushed to make the change? Who's going to raise the heat to drive change? Who's going to carry out the change?

Well, who has made everything that's good in this country? Who did the work that, at times, brought about some of the most secure middle-income people in history? Who also did all the work that enabled the powerful to become powerful? Who is capable of creating the great change we need? And who is it who has to be the ones to do it? The only ones in the picture who can really determine how things go? Who is the country of, who is it by, who is it for, who is responsible for having let it wander off track, who has to fix what's broken in it, and who are the only ones with the power and the ability to do that? US.

Of, by, for, responsible for fixes, and with the power to shape it. US. Always was US. Always is US. Only US.

How

There's no need for analyzing and agonizing over how impossible it is to get big change moving, or how we could ever possibly counter the power of the powerful. That's all distraction and foggy thinking. It's all a paper-thin illusion we've gradually allowed ourselves to think we are walled in by. The moment we flip that mental switch and declare that, when it comes to change, when it comes to how things run, it's all on US, and now we're going to make the change happen, it will. Once we make that decision, to then wonder whether the change will really happen makes no more sense than to wonder, once you start walking, will you be walking? It's happening. The nation is whatever our choices and our work make it to be.

We're good at working, building wealth, building other things of value like families and local cultures and wonderful mixes of varied cultures and communities, building national highways systems and every other such thing we need, and finding ever better ways to be good stewards. We've let ourselves be conned into getting a little off track, but we're able to get a handle on that too. We've made the nation favor our interests before. It can be done now. After all, we're not just talking about any group to do it. We're talking about a group who has the power, the proven ability, and the work results to show. A group who is perfect for the job. US.

Notes

From Our Hands

Simple early space capsule
airandspace.si.edu/multimedia-gallery/friendship7jpg
airandspace.si.edu/stories/editorial/getting-closer-look-
mercury-friendship-7-spacecraft

Early creating of silicon designs
www.iuma.ulpgc.es/~lopez/articulos/fairchild.pdf

Taping a circuit board
www.industrial-electronics.com/eed5th_5.html

Velcro and Microwave
www.popularmechanics.com/science/health/g1216/10-
awesome-accidental-discoveries/

Working Peoples' Share

The standard, commonly accepted measurement of how the pie
is sliced between labor and capital, that is, between working

peoples' income versus the investment income (investment is mostly how the wealthy get their income), is what the Federal Reserve calls the "Share of Labour Compensation" and the Bureau of Labor Statistics (BLS) calls the "Labor Share of Output". They calculate this by tracking measures of labor compensation and measures of investment income and comparing the two. It's not an exact number since some income is hard to categorize, but it is a measure that virtually all economists have a high degree of confidence in. Ideas have been suggested at times on how to make it slightly more accurate, but for the purposes here they don't matter. All versions of the measurement show the same declines of labor share over the same time frames. The share had been on a steady decline since shortly after World War II, with various minor ups and downs as the economy went up and down but still on an overall decline. Then with the recession of 2001 it took a much bigger dive and continued that rapid fall long after that recession ended, and it still had just barely stopped falling when the recession of 2008 hit. Again the recovery took an extraordinarily long time to begin to help wages. As of 2019 it had started to go up a little, due to the economy having gradually reached a good state, but the likelihood is that that will only last until the next downturn, when the overall falling will continue.

Bureau of Labor Statistics, Labor Share data
www.bls.gov/opub/ted/2017/labor-share-of-output-has-declined-since-1947.htm

Wall St Journal quote
www.wsj.com/articles/despite-tight-job-market-labor-forces-income-is-squeezed-11550930400

The Two Pay Systems

Studies showing to what extent raising wages raises prices.

ftp.iza.org/dp1072.pdf

fee.org/articles/what-the-minimum-wage-does-to-food-prices-and-job-hiring/

www.marketwatch.com/story/raising-fast-food-hourly-wages-to-15-would-raise-prices-by-4-study-finds-2015-07-28

As the studies show, if a burger joint paid burger flippers $10 an hour, and the burger flippers demanded and got a raise to $11 an hour, then the joint's big $5 burger would rise to $5.20. There are lots of expenses and factors in the cost of running a business and setting prices, besides wages, though wages are a big part. But raising wages does not raise prices to the point where it cancels out, to where your cost of living goes up so much that it eats up all of your raise. Consider that burger flipper. Their wage went up 10 percent but the cost of a burger only went up 4 percent. Raising wages will raise prices but not nearly so much that it cancels out.

Wage Theft

General information on wage theft
www.alternet.org/2019/03/waging-war-on-wage-theft/

Notes

The dollar volume of wage theft
www.epi.org/publication/employers-steal-billions-from-workers-paychecks-each-year/

New delivery companies using apps make tip unclear and deliverer might not get it
www.vox.com/the-goods/2019/4/24/18513559/tipping-policies-doordash-instacart-amazon-flex-new-york-bill

List of largest corporations with largest wage theft fines
www.goodjobsfirst.org/sites/default/files/docs/pdfs/wagetheft_report_revised.pdf

Made in the USA
Coppell, TX
01 August 2020

32105227R00075